THE
SELF-EMPOWERMENT
Journal

REVISED EDITION

KARAMOKOH B. WURIE

CONTENTS

Chapter 1: Developing The Mindset 1

Tab 1:   Your First Job 5

Tab 2:   Paradigm 24

Tab 3:   Financial thermostat 27

Tab 4:   Thoughts 29

Tab 5:   Faith 31

Tab 6:   Affirmations 34

Tab 7:   Gratitude 35

Tab 8:   Act as if or Simulate 36

Tab 9:   The sub-conscious and the Conscious mind 39

Tab 10: Energy 42

Tab 11: The one-day theory and time 47

Tab 12: What is your Why? 50

Tab 13: Action 52

Tab 14: Our Belief System 54

Tab 15: Problems or Trial and Tribulation 56

Tab 16: Find Inspiration 57

Tab 17: The Elite Laws 60

Tab 18: The World is just like a computer 63

Tab 19: Debts 64

Tab 20: The Power of Asking 66

Tab 21: Focus on Expansion 67

Tab 22: Be above average 68

Tab 23:   Your Haters are Your Angels............................ 69

Tab 24:   Your Relationship With God or High Power................. 71

Chapter 2: Start your own business...........................73

Tab 25:   Online Business 76

Tab 26:   Start Right Now.. 79

Tab 27:   Research Your Ideas 81

Tab 28:   Identify Your Buyer... 82

Tab 29:   Develop Your Product or Service................................. 83

Tab 30:   Use Leverage 86

Tab 31:   Showcase Your Business 88

Tab 32:   Business Launch... 95

Tab 33:   Your First One Million...................................... 99

AUTO BIOGRAPH

Karamokoh Wurie was Born in Free Town, Sierra Leone, West Africa. Growing up in Sierra Leone was such a harsh and humbling experience for Karamokoh: "I remember the times when we would have dinner. I would try my hardest not to finish my food, all in one sitting. I would want to save some for the next day, because the next meal may not come in two, three days or so. That used to be a tough choice, knowing how good the food tasted. "But you always have to think of the next day," as my mother used to say. Perhaps it was one of my older cousin's advice that helped me out the most. He would suggest that we drank a lot of water after each meal so that we would get full quicker and the meal would last longer in our stomach. That idea seemed very good at the time but not on school week when I had to walk on foot for about 30 minutes on that dusty, rugged road to school.

Walking that length of a distance in the hot sun, while having a stomach partially full of water was not always the right choice. That was partly one of the things that were making me late for school sometimes. Being late to school was also consequential because I would get a serious beaten by my teachers for not getting to school on time. This snapshot of my life was the norm while growing up in Sierra Leone until the civil war took place, then everything went a little more chaos. Even though somehow we survived that war, but it was excruciating to come back to a burnt down-home and had to clean up and started over.

After we made it through all those painful conditions, I was fortunate enough to have been brought to the United States. December 1999, that was the year that I arrived in the US. Things were a little better in the States compare to Sierra Leone. I didn't have to walk to school anymore. I never had to get beaten by my teachers. We stayed in Alexandria, Virginia. In Virginia, I attended Sixth grade at the Bucknell Elementary school. I attended Carl Sandburg Middle and West Potomac High School."

After High school, in 2007, Karamokoh started attending Virginia Commonwealth University. During his first year of college, things didn't pan out too well for him. Karamokoh was working two jobs, while also going to college. He ended up finding himself in multiple debts and so much struggle.

In 2009, Karamokoh enlisted into the army to become part of the 92Y, Quartermaster. His assigned units and duty station include the 36th Engineer Brigade in Fort Hood, Texas. The 214th Aviation Battalion in Wiesbaden, Germany. The 16th Military Police Brigade, and the 83rd Civil Affairs Battalion in Fort Bragg, North Carolina.

Karamokoh was deployed twice to Afghanistan in support of "Operation Enduring Freedom," and was also part of the detail team that provided support for the "Anakonda 16" exercise that took place in Poland.

Karamokoh has been awarded an Army Commendation Medal, 3 Army Achievement, 3 Army Good Conduct Medals, one National Defense Service Medal, two Afghan Campaign Medals, one Global War on Terrorism Medal, One National Defense, one None Commission Officer Professional Developmental Ribbon, one Army Service Ribbon, one Oversea Service Ribbon, and one Nato Medal.

DISCLAIMER

Please understand that the author of this book is not a financial or a medical adviser. The author wrote this book for informational purposes only. This book was not written on the premises to solve individuals' legal, financial, tax, psychological, and emotional problems. The information outlined in this book is based on the author's point of view and his interpretation of things based on his experience, education, and observational standpoint. It's up to the reader to accept or reject such information. It's not the author's intent to convince the reader to accept or believe in a particular religion.

DEDICATION

I dedicate this book to my high school teacher Ms. Angela Brisbane who became my mother after letting me stay in her basement when I was still trying to figure things out.

In early 2008, during the economic recession, things were tough for me. I was laid off from my job, and I had just lost my car in an accident. I was overdue on my rent. I was failing some of my classes in college. I remember that afternoon standing in the school library starring out the window, feeling lost and helpless. I decided to get on the computer to check my email. Just out of the blue, I got the most encouraging and uplifting email from Ms. Brisbane, without her knowing my current situation at the time. After reading that email, it changed my mental state. I regained my strength, and I was able to push forward and came up with a solution for the situations that I was going through. I truly appreciate all that you've done for me.

INTRODUCTION

This book is practical. Read the content of this book in a digestive manner. Steady take small bits of the information outlined in the book and reflect upon it to get a deeper understanding and to start developing a mind transformation, before moving on to the next idea. I also encourage you to research some of the topics, ideas or people mentioned in this book. There are only two chapters or two parts to this book. Chapter one is mainly to reprogram your mind to discover you, the real you. Chapter two break down other avenues or approaches that you can take to gain financial freedom, as opposed to settling for the status quo or going with the flow.

As you continue to read this book, throughout, you'll notice the word "Elite" appear a lot of times. My goal was to use this word so many times that it would stay in your subconscious mind. I wanted to make sure that by the end of this book, from the information that you are getting and the in-depth understanding of this information, you should have developed an elite state of mind. This is to raise your vibration and to uplift you! Remember, words are very powerful.

Another thing that you may notice from reading this book is that I used some high dollar numbers in all the commercial examples used in this book. I want you to become very acquainted with high-value figures. My goal with this was to help shift your Paradigm and raise your financial thermostat.

CHAPTER 1

DEVELOPING THE MINDSET

Wednesday, November 28, 2018. 3:30 AM.

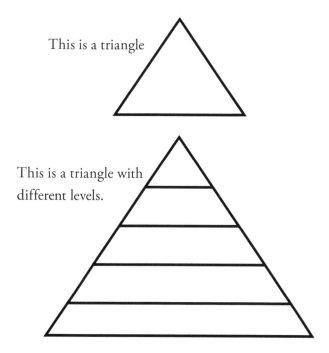

This is a triangle

This is a triangle with different levels.

Even though I haven't met you yet but I guarantee that you are most likely somewhere in this triangle. You've probably been in this triangle for almost your whole life. Whether you are a Doctor, Lawyer, teacher, student, you are somewhere in this triangle. It doesn't matter what your occupation is, and you are most likely in this triangle. Even if you are unemployed, you are somewhat in this triangle. If you are trying to lose weight, you are probably in this triangle. If you are looking for a job, you are in this triangle. Being in this triangle applies to almost everything that you are trying to do in life. There is nothing wrong with being in the triangle, but you don't want to be lost or get stuck in it. You want to think outside of the triangle first before getting into it. The whole time you've been in this triangle, your essential focus is to continue climbing up to the next level or to get to the highest point. The thing is, you are not even sure if making it to the next level or being at the top of this triangle is what you truly want, but it's human nature to always want to strive for improvement.

You may be asking how or why am I in this triangle? Well, the whole triangle thing is a metaphor. The point that I was trying to make is that. For one, most people never **thought** of **prescribing** their ideal life in-terms of these five major components: health, wealth, love, spirituality, and creativity. Some people may have thought of this, but never **acted** upon it.

Another point that I'm trying to make is that most people don't believe that those five principal components are attainable or it all possible for them. It is why most people have been going with the flow. If you can be honest with yourself right now, ask yourself, why are you doing what you are doing. Why are you applying for that job? Why are you trying to get promoted? Why are you trying to lose that weight? Why are you trying to date that boy or girl? Why are you going to school? You are most likely applying for that job because it has more to offer than what you currently already have. In other words, you are trying to move to a different level up in the triangle. The same goes for trying to get promoted, lose weight, going to school, etc. I can almost guarantee that at some point in your life, you've told yourself the following: "I want to live in such and such," "I want to gain or lose x amount of weight." "I want to be an Astronaut, a doctor, a lawyer, etc.," or whatever the case may have been for you. There is nothing wrong with all this, except it only focusing on one anchor point of your life. You must change your way of thinking and get rid of that triangular mindset, and then everything will start to flow.

You want to be in the circle where everything flows and continues to circulate. The circle is where you have balance. It is also where you have your perfect life in terms of the five major components of life that I mentioned above. I called this circle, the circle of life, or COL for short. You can use the triangle to get you into the COL. The problem with most people is that they wait until they get to the top of the triangle, or a couple of levels up before they would want to create their circle of life. Some people only focus on one or two areas of their COL, and this creates a void in the other regions. Concentrating on only a few aspects of your COL creates an unbalanced life. A visual way to describe this is to imagine an Airplane in the sky with one wing missing. Sooner or later, it would be very shaky, spiral out of control, and eventually crash. If you are reading this, please don't be like a one-winged airplane. Have both of your wings, so that you can soar!

Some people wait until they get that perfect job, that promotion, etc. before they can start thinking or creating their ideal life. Even worse, sometimes they don't even think of creating their perfect lifestyle, they steadily keep going blind-fully. People do what they feel is right or what they've seen others done. If you are experiencing this, it is not your fault. Nobody was given a road map with all the steps on how to live a life entirely. The reason why you keep gaining back that weight, or why you keep going back to that addiction is because you've only thought to go one level from where you are currently. You have not entirely made up your mind to reach your COL. When you have clarity and determination of where you want to be in life (the circle), then you can walk up that triangle with no problem. Now keep in mind that it takes focus, determination, and some other crucial principles (that I would talk about further down this book) to reach your COL.

You may have heard people say things like, "I'm going to lose x-pounds this Summer," or "I'm going to apply for that job." Remember, there is nothing wrong with that, but it is just an anchor point, or it's only focusing on one aspect of your COL. It is hard to succeed in just one area of your COL, while the other areas are lacking. Identify what you want. You want to create a sustainable, balanced lifestyle. You must do this with a lot of forward-thinking. Find a quiet place. Think of the kind of lifestyle that you would want to have. Write down anything that comes into your mind. Think of what would your day to day look like. What kind of things would you be doing? How would you feel once you achieve this kind of lifestyle? Please take this very seriously. Use your imagination. **Think** and **prescribe** your ideal life in-terms of those five significant components mentioned above, then start **acting** upon them. Your daily activity should contribute to each one of those five components. As you can tell, the words "**think** or **thought**, **prescribe**, and **act** written in bold. It is because those are the main ingredients for creating your ideal life. All the other instruments that I am going to talk about further down this book are just mechanics of those main ingredients. For example, I am going to talk about having faith further down. **Acting** or taking action on something also illustrates belief or faith.

I mentioned the five major components of creating your ideal life like health, wealth, spirituality, and creativity. These are the five major components of life because every other area of life falls around those. For example, recreational can fall under creativity. Freedom can be wealth, etc.

TAB **1**

Your First Job

The first thing that I want to talk about is your first job. A lot of people never worked their first job, and this is one of the main reasons why most people are still working unfulfilling jobs. There isn't any specific qualification, or any primary requirement needed to start your first job. You don't need to be a certain age, and you don't need to have any special skills. All you need is the guts or the willingness to start. So…, let me ask you this question. Do you have the desire to start your first job today? If you've answered yes to this question, well congratulation elite, you just got hired. Clock in, and you can start working on your first job today. Elite your first job is YOU.

You are your primary employer. You should've started working on yourself before you work at any other occupation. Work on yourself spiritually, mentally, and physically. When you've fully mastered yourself, then life can be seamless. You'll discard most of your victim mentality. You'll also notice that it's not the economy that holds you back from living your best life. It's not the president, your boss, your neighbor, etc. Elite, you are the center of your reality. As you continue to read this book, I'm going to guide you through the process of starting your first job.

Here are steps that you can take right now to begin your first job:

STEP 1: Stop right now where you are. Take five minutes to examine where you currently are in life. Bring all your attention to this present moment. Ask yourself, is this the life you had wanted for yourself? Do you feel like you deserve more? Two main reasons why you are where you are right now. Reason number one is because you've been thinking very small.

Reason number two is because of the story you've been telling yourself. You may have said things like: "I'm going to try and get a job so that I can be able to pay my rent." A couple of years later, you found yourself doing just that, working to pay the rent. Your way of thinking and your internal stories are the contributing factors to your current reality. We live in a universe of possibilities. Think of your mind as a gear. Whenever you concentrate your thinking onto something, your mind starts shifting into gear. As the gear shifts, it'll begin to bring you closer to the possibilities of the things that you've concentrated your mind. Get a clear and bigger picture of where you want your life to be. Write it on a paper, and this will connect your mind and your thoughts and helps to solidify. Determine your COL and write a new story of your life.

STEP 2: You must know this one single truth. No matter where you are in life right now, know that you're capable. You were also meant to be prosperous and flourish. Unrealizing this truth may lead to an unpleasant lifestyle. Almost everything that you are going to read in this book is rooted back to this one simple fact. I don't know where your life is right now. You may be living pay-check to pay-check, but the fact remains that you are meant to prosper.

You may be working at a job where you feel very inadequate. You may have co-workers that look down on you. You may feel like life is just pointless, and you just can't get anything right. You may be in debt. You may be homeless, you may have been cheated on, all your friends may be fake and backstabbing, but just know that you were meant to prosper! No matter what the circumstance is, no matter what the situation is, just know that you were meant for greatness. So smile, Elite, smile.

STEP 3: Trust in the fact that you meant for greatness. Go to sleep every day, knowing and believing in this fact. Wake up every morning, knowing and understanding in this fact. Go into every situation, knowing and believing in this fact.

STEP 4: Know that you can be in control of your destiny. Have this belief in both your conscious and your subconscious mind. Hold on to this idea no matter what, and hold yourself accountable. As you read further down this book, I will discuss some more principal instruments that'll help shape your destiny.

STEP 5: Now, Elite, I want you to ask yourself this question: "who am I really?" and try to notice what kind of answers that'll come up in your mind. Know that you are not just your name, your race, your job title, and so on. Let your mind investigate the answer. Reject any limiting thinking such as "I am my name." "I am my occupation," "I am such and such ethnicity," "I am this race, "etc. Those are limiting answers to who you indeed are. Those answers only describe you on the surface level. They are also just external identifications that have been placed on you by yourself and others. As an Elite, you want to get a deeper reflection of who you legitimately are, allow your mind to separate YOU from your body. After you've mindfully detached yourself from your body, then you'll be able to plant whatever new image you may want for yourself. Trust me, Elite. You are an unlimited being that can do anything! As I've mentioned before, gaining this realization is the first part of discovering YOURSELF.

Think of a professional Soccer player who got excellent soccer skills. Now imagine that same Soccer player in an Astronaut suit trying to play soccer. That Soccer player would have less versatility in the Astronaut suit because the suit would create some limitations for him or her. Does this mean that the Professional soccer player lacks the same athleticism that he or she had before putting on the outfit? Would the soccer player realize that he or she is capable of doing those fantastic maneuvering techniques? Or is he or she limited to only what they can do while wearing the Astronaut suit? That example is a similar representation of YOU and your body. You are an unlimited spirit; energy stuck in a suit, your body. Always remember that you are a non-physical being or a soul. You live on a physical plane. To experience and interact with this material world, you were given a physical body. You body was only for the interactual purpose to keep you in this this physical plane or to keep you safe during your time here on earth. What I am saying is don't let gravity hold you back. Jump for the moon, Elite!

STEP 6: Elite, where do you see yourself three years from now? This question may sound very familiar to you. It's one of the issues that most students have asked to answer. You've probably been asked this question by your teachers, parents, or even at your current job. A lot of times, when you ask people this question, they try to come up with answers that sound good to the person who is asking the question. Other times when people are facing this question, they try to come up with one single answer, and the answer is usually related to their jobs or career. Sometimes people also assess their current situation to answer this question. Consequently, they'll tell you where they think that they will be, and not really where their more significant potential would take them.

Teacher: Where do you see yourself three years from now, Bob?

Bob: (Without that much thought or consideration), "Three years from now, I will be working for XYZ corporation." "Three years from now, I will be the CEO of XYZ corporation." "Three years from now, I will start my own XYZ business." "Uuuuh, I don't know. I've never thought about where I would be three years from now."

It is not to say that Bob's answers are not good enough. The problem is that they are missing some other vital elements. The key to answering this question is that it should come deep from your heart. It should be in the form of a narrative with a deeper reflection. Know that your current situation does not determine where you will be three years from now. To better answer this question, you may want to refer back to the five major components of life that I talked about at the beginning of this book. As you answer this question, you want to make sure it at least covers these areas: health, wealth, and happiness. Also think in terms of your hobbies, friendship, family and believe that wherever you see yourself three years from now, you may get there. Please do not just try to come up with a simple Bob answer.

Imagine that you can have whatever you ask or say. Three years from now, what will your day to day resemble? Think outside of your current life. Stretch your imagination as you answer this question. There is no right or wrong answer to this, but you want to make it to what you truly want in life. Think, if money is not an issue, not having any talent is no issue, if your race, religion, is not an issue, where would you see yourself three years from now? Imagine if whatever answer that you can come up with right now is where you'll see yourself three years from now. What would your answer be?

Do not be afraid to think big, because bigger goals and dreams are inspiring, and they will stimulate your mind to act creatively. You will continue to see this concept further down as you continue to read this book. The whole idea of this is for you to have a clear vision of the kind of lifestyle that you truly desire, and know that you deserve it!

Here is another way to view this concept. Imagine getting in your car to go someplace. You know exactly where you want to go, and you'll continue to drive until you get there. Your whole purpose of being in that car is to get to a destination. This entire concept applies to your life. Once you have clarity of what you want with your life, then you've given your life real purpose and meaning. A life with a purpose is fascinating. Having a clear goal in life, and owning up to it will make it a lot easier to navigate through. Otherwise, you could be living in the wrong perception.

CHECKPOINT 1:

-Close your eyes and repeat these phrases in your mind:

I am powerful!

I have an abundance!

I am healthy!

I am wealthy!

I feel great!

I look great!

-Write these phrases down in your journal

-Read these phrases out loud.

-Strongly believe those above statements!

EXERCISE 1
JOURNAL ENTRY: RE-DEFINE YOUR LIFE'S PURPOSE:

Get yourself a journal book. For the sake of this exercise, imagine that you can have whatever you are going to write on this journal page entry. Pretend this will all come true because it will. Where would you want to see yourself three years from now? Think about the kind of experiences that you would like to have, the type of places that you would like to go to and the sort of things that you would like to do or have. Be very specific as you write this in your journal book. Do not worry about the mechanical aspect of how you are going to get there. Only focus on the end state of where you want to be. You see, there are two points in life at any given intervals of your choice. Point A: is where you are right now, and point B: is where you want to be in the future period of your choosing. Everything else in-between is just actionable steps that are going to get you to point B. Your actionable steps must be in alignment with your point B. You want to examine your current Point A and clearly define your Point B, then start connecting the line from point A to point B. The line between point A and point B is the journey or the process. Once you've clearly defined your Point B, you want to make sure you enjoy the journey or the process that is going to get you there. The day that you arrive at your Point B, it now becomes your other new point A, so you must redefine another new point B. Your other new point B should always be ambiguous than your other new point A. It should also be an increase or shows growth and maturity from your new point A. Do not let yourself be in stagnation. You always want to continue to create and excel. Stagnation is boring and can cause your life to be miserable.

KARAMOKOH B. WURIE

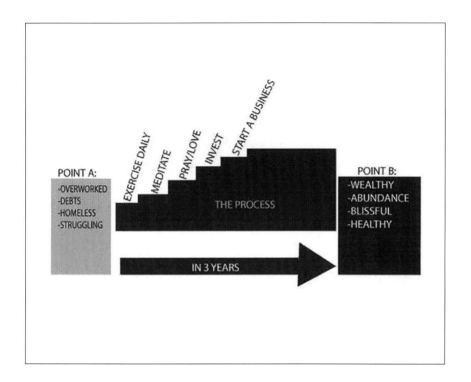

Life is not a destination, it's a journey, but we must continue plotting new locations as we move forward. It will continue to pull us through the process. Creating a perspective time-based destination gives you sort of a roadmap that you could use to navigate through. Elite, as you continue this voyage of life, having excess baggage is a hassle. It can slow you down or crippled you from reaching your plotted location of where you want to be. Therefore, on the next exercise, we are going to go through a process of psychological transformation. It is where you are going to drop off all those unnecessary baggage. You see, some of the things that stop people from achieving greatness, are worries, regrets, doubts, procrastination, fear, uncertainty, etc. Follow the exercise down below to see how you can start transforming your mind.

> ## CHECKPOINT 2:
> **-Close your eyes and repeat these phrases in your mind:**
>> I am powerful!
>>
>> I have an abundance!
>>
>> I am healthy!
>>
>> I am wealthy!
>>
>> I feel great!
>>
>> I look great!
>
> **-Write these phrases down in your journal**
>
> **-Read these phrases out loud.**
>
> **-Strongly believe those above statements!**

EXERCISE 2
STARTING NEW

Get a blank piece of paper. Assuming that you may already have setbacks, or you are just not where you want to be in life. Come up with a generalized title for all your stumbling blocks, or the things have been holding you back from achieving success. Write the title at the top of the paper in big, bold letters. For instance, you could think of something that you would love to do and then think of all the negative beliefs that have stopped you from doing it. These may be things like time, fear, doubts, excuses, regrets, "I'm too old," I'm not good enough, "and so on. Whatever the case may be for you, try to make your title a little painful if you can. Doing this reminds the subconscious mind that it's something that doesn't serve you, and you'll need to get rid of it. Here are some examples of titles that you may use:

"ALL MY REGRETS," "MY GREATEST SETBACKS,"

"ALL MY GRUDGES,"

"THE PEOPLE I HATE,"

"MY BIGGEST MISTAKES IN LIFE,"

"THINGS THAT MAKE ME A FAILURE,"
"THINGS THAT STOPPED ME FROM BECOMING A PROFESSIONAL ATHLETE." etc.

Once you have your title, then start writing down all your mistakes, grudges, doubts, fear, regrets, or things you wish you could go back in time and change. Take your time with this. Take an entire day if you have to. You can do this whole process more than once. For some people, it may be harder to let go on the first try. Whenever you start to feel stuck in life, you can always come back and repeat this exercise. It takes repeating for things to register in the subconscious mind. As you do this exercise, believe in your intellect that you are willing to let this go today and start a new slate. Start re-stating all your regrets out loud, then either before or after that, add the phrase "I wish to let this go today!" "this no longer serves me!" or think of any other letting go phrase that you may know. After you complete this, then crumple the piece of paper (with all your regrets, grudges, doubts, or fear) and burn it. This action shows your subconscious mind that you are getting rid of all the negative things that have held you back. If you are not able to burn the paper, put it in a shredder, or crumple it and throw it in the trash.

Here is an example

MY BIGGEST DOWNFALL

-I regret not going to college
-I wish I could have avoided that car accident
-I wish I had a father
-My highschool teacher told me that I would always be a failure in life
-My own parents told me that am worthless
-I should have never married that guy or girl
_I am too fat too be a model
-Time is just passing me by
-I'm too old to start...
-If I didn't have any children, I would...

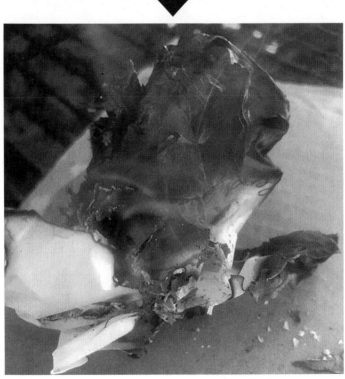

Next, use Microsoft word, or a paper and a red marker. Write this statement with your name: "My name is_____," underneath that, write or type up to four powerful statements in big, bold letters that are true, or you would like to be true about yourself. Take that piece of paper with those statements and frame it. Frame it in your living room, in your office, or somewhere you most likely to see it regularly. Read this out loud every morning, or whenever you are having a bad day. Read this statement out loud with power, with secure believing, read it and start feeling like you are unstoppable and on top of the world, because you are!

STEP 7: As you continue to go through the process of developing this elite state of mind, you'll have to work on yourself physically, mentally, and spiritually. Your health is also essential. Get in the habit of drinking a cold glass of water as soon as you get out of bed and ensure that you drink an adequate amount of water throughout the day. Eat fruits and vegetables as part of your daily healthy diet. Start your day with some physical exercises. Physical exercises are not only good for the body, but it also enhances your mental faculties. By now, you should already have a journal book. It is where you will document all your feelings, goals, ideas, and so on. As you continue with your transformation, you'll notice new ideas would start showing up in your mind. Use your journal to record all your thoughts. Start filling your brain up with vast knowledge and positivity. Begin making it a habit to read books on self-development. There are many written materials and audiobooks on this subject. All of this may sound very minute and simplistic, but doing the little things now will help you achieve the more important things later. As you continue to renew your mind, try to align it with your action and your environment.

Elite, It's not the big mansion that we want; instead, it's the feeling of having that mansion is what we truly want. Imagine having a big mansion but not feel very happy about it; this makes having the mansion unimportant. Start creating those good feelings today. Make your bed when you wake up in the morning. Tidy up your place. Have your things organized and act as if you are already living in a big fancy mansion. Make sure that your home is always smelling good. Start taking good care of where you are living right now as if it is your dream place. It is how you prime yourself for success; it also shows that you are in control of your life and not the other way around. It will create an excellent feeling, and it would help you have a clear mental space. Be appreciative of the things you already have by taking good care of them. Start gradually living today, the type of lifestyle you want to live tomorrow. Treat yourself every once in a while. Find a time in the day where you have to declutter your mind.

Pray to a higher power, or to yourself, the universe, etc. You can also

just set aside a few minutes of the day for meditation and visualization —
meditation for peace of mind and the healing of the mind, body, and soul.
One of the simplest ways to do meditation is to Find a quiet, comfortable
place. Sit or lay down with your body very relaxed. Close your eyes. Take
three deep breaths at 30 seconds interval each then try to quiet your mind.
Focus and center your mind in the present. Try to deflect any negative
thoughts that may arise or let them drift away. Feel that inner sense of peace.
Know that everything is going to be alright, and you are in control. Know
that you are powerful. Center yourself and embrace that good feeling from
the meditation. You can also use guided meditation audios. You can find
these audios on YouTube.

Practice doing visualization, as well. Visualization is the same process
as meditation. Make sure you are at a quiet, comfortable place, with your
body relaxed, and have taken three deep refreshing breaths. Close your eyes
and try to visualize your ideal lifestyle vividly. Use visualization to foresee
the kind of life that you would like to live. Use your imagination as you
keep your eyes closed. See yourself where you would like your life to to be.
Go to that place in your imagination. Try to picture every detail such as
texture, smell, atmosphere. For example, you maybe sitting in your private
jet. What does the seats feel like? What kind of materials are they made
off? You should combine your visuals with actualization. Actualization is
when you start living your imagination in real life— by doing some of the
things that can help bring your vision into fruition. For example, if you
visualize yourself to be a football coach, then go start volunteering at a
local Elementary school to be the kids' football coach. Be sure to be very
specific in your imagination about your ideal lifestyle; know what you
want and start speaking it into existence.

Words are powerful, just like your imagination. Do not speak contrary
to yourself or others. You'll give life to your ideal life by talking about
it. The ways you talk about it also count. Talk in the present tense. Talk
as if you've already got it. Talk about it with joy and passion. Do not be
like most people who say things like, "I want to be the only one in my

family to graduate college," unless that's what you really and only want. There is nothing wrong with that statement, but there should be more to it. For instance, that same statement should be restated in the following: "I am going to be the only one in my family who graduated college. Top of my class, at XYZ University, and become the chairman at the XYZ corporation, making X amount of dollars a year…" Always try to include definiteness, purpose, and passion whenever you speak of your future. Doing this will add fuel to your imagination. I will touch more on visualization further down in this book.

STEP 8: Apply the same effort on yourself as you would at any other job. Elite, be very disciplined. The same way that you would set the alarm just to drag yourself to go to some job is the same way you should work on yourself if not better. Always pur yourself first! You are the most valuale person you would ever have to deal with.

Next, start giving yourself awards and recognitions! Start setting small goals for yourself and reward yourself each time you achieve them. You have the power to start validating yourself at the highest degree possible. Do not wait for anyone else to do this for you. Give yourself a certificate of completion, or a certificate of achievement, and other awards for each time you complete a self-set goal. You can invite friends and families to these self-directed award ceremonies. You can host these ceremonies at your home, your local restaurants, the park, etc. After you complete reading this book with all the activities in it. You shuld go to your local Office Depot and have a certificate of completion made for you with your name on it.

I know that this may sound very silly, but these little things count as a way of self-empowering yourself and preparing yourself for the future. It's funny how some people are so desperate for notoriety from others rather themselves. For example, being in the army, we usually get awarded for achieving a particular milestone. I remember one time I got a specific award, and there was a guy in my unit that didn't get this award. The guy had a lot of resentment because he felt like he did the most and deserved that award. For my part, even though I appreciated that award but it wouldn't have made a big difference about how I felt if I wouldn't have gotten it. I always viewed awards as just a piece of paper with just fancy words on it. I felt awful for that guy. I did Graphic Design at the time, so I even thought of making the same award for him. As I've continued to self-develop myself, I found it very strange to see people get very excited from the validation that they get from others. Still, those people never take the time to validate themselves.

STEP 9: Start aligning yourself with like-minded people. It will help strengthen you. You want to surround yourself with people that will empower you. There are different networking events where you can meet people of the same interests. You'll read more about these later on. Stay away from negative and pessimistic people. Elite, you'll start to attract these negative attributes if you don't distance yourself from them. As you continue to fill yourself up with all this positivity and raising your conscious mind, you'll start noticing all the negativity that you weren't probably aware of before. It would start to make you feel very uncomfortable. Try not to engage too much of your mind into non-productive activities like visiting celebrities gossiping websites or social media pages. Instead, try to fill up your mind with motivational and inspirational stories.

STEP 10: Create your circle of life or your ideal lifestyle. Get a piece of paper or use your journal. Draw a big circle and write in it your desired perfect life. Don't be afraid to think big! Think in- terms of the five major components of life that I mentioned earlier. Draw a triangle underneath the circle. In the triangle, jot down the steps, or the things that must occur for you to reach your circle of life. Next, you would want to create what I called a power To-do list, daily. Most people create a To-do list about a week out or the night before. The thing that I found about that strategy is that it is kind of stale, or I usually end up forgetting about it.

Elite, you want to create a power to-do list every day before you go about your day. Your to-do list should be of what you are going to accomplish for that day, not the next day, not next week or in the future. You should have a fixed number of tasks on your to-do list every day. You want to keep your to-do list very fresh. Every day before you go out of your day, you should create your Power to-do list of the things that you are trying to accomplish for that day. If there are things that you couldn't get accomplished on that day, be sure to include them when you write your new power to-do list the next day. Using this strategy can be very exciting and motivating. Alright, let's run through the entire process one more time just to get clarity. Soon as you wake up in the morning after you've completed your daily meditations, affirmations, and visualizations. Find a quiet place and list the things that you are going to accomplish on that same day. Make sure those things are aligning to that triangle, which is also aligning to your circle of life. Try to include the five major components of life as part of your daily to-do list.

Having a daily power to-do list keeps you focused and very structured. Have your power to-do list someplace where you can see it regularly throughout the day, glance at it every moment that you get. If you have your Power to-do list in a journal book, have that page always open throughout the day. For example, I always put my power to-do list on the front passenger seat of my car. Anytime I come to a traffic stop. I would grab my Power to-do

list to take a glance at it. I use it to determine my workflow for the day. You should be able to create a balanced optimal life using this strategy. With this, you know exactly where you are going, and you know what to do. You don't have to start looking for answers someplace else. The power to-do list can help equational your success. Before I started using the Power to-do list, I was always worried if I was on the right track. I was always very tempted to jump on to the next business venture. I felt lost, and I even hired a personal life coach. It wasn't until I started using my power to-do list that I developed the stagnated clarity and a sense of direction. Here is another example and a break down on how to get this process done: First, you are going to draw a circle. In this circle, you are going to Prescribe your ideal lifestyle. Think in terms of the five major components of life. Next, you are going to draw a triangle and list all the practical steps that you are going to take to get to your circle. You'll use your Power to-do list as a tool to map out your everyday micro-steps in alignment with your COL.

STEP 11: Make a firm declaration to yourself that you will reach your purpose and reach your destiny in life. Go in front of the mirror and look yourself deep in your eyes to see God who dwells in you. See the fearless, the strongest, and the bravest human being that you are. After you see yourself, your deeper self, the mighty you, then you are going to start pounding on your chest and shout out loud the following truth phrases. "I have God in me!" "I am powerful!" "I can do all things!" "I am unstoppable!" "I was made perfect!" "I will flourish!" "I will reach my destiny!" "I will live a purposeful life!"

Elite, you can do this more than once if you need to. Make sure you do this with power, purpose, conviction, and motivation. What this is going to do is that it is going to invoke the Spirit in you. The Spirit of persistence, the Spirit of breakthrough that is in you. This will also help to put your mind in a much more dominant state. It will give you the will-power to be able to conquer the day. Elite for at least the next 21 days, this is the first thing that you would want to do as soon as you wake up. Each day that you wake up is a blessing, so own each day. Wake up with power and excitement. As you continue to do this, and as time goes by, the Spirit in you may die down depending on what life throws at you. For any time you fall off, start back over, and make a new declaration. Elite, you will continue to do this until you complete 21 consecutive days. It has been said that it takes at least 21 days to develop a new habit. Even though this may not be a clear-cut or the end all be all, but you can use it as a baseline to help strengthen you.

CHECKPOINT 3:

-Close your eyes and repeat these phrases in your mind:

    I am powerful!

    I have an abundance!

    I am healthy!

    I am wealthy!

    I feel great!

    I look great!

-Write these phrases down in your journal

-Read these phrases out loud.

-Strongly believe in the above statements!

EXERCISE 3
SET A GOAL THAT YOU WOULD LIKE TO ACCOMPLISH IN THE NEXT 3 WEEKS.

Goal setting takes focus, energy, action, discipline, commitment, and accountability. When I first set out to write this book, it first started as a simple journal entry. Later, I was inspired to write it into a book. Initially, when I first started, it took me a couple of months off and on to write just a few pages, as I was working on other things. I was also very distracted and wasn't fully committed. About two weeks ago, I made it a commitment to finish this book this month. I set everything else aside. It became my main focus. I think about the completion of this book almost every hour of the day. I concentrated all my energy on the fruition of this book. I envisioned the finished product. I was holding the physical copy of the book and flipping through the pages in my mind. I visualized what I wanted the book cover to be. I woke up early in the mornings and tried to spend some hours into writing this book before I go to work.

I held myself accountable. I cut off other distractions, like; watching TV, etc. It wasn't until after all this, I became very empowered, and I was able to speed up the process. Within a couple of days, I was able to write way more pages for this book than I have done over the past couple of months. All of a sudden, it just becomes a breeze, and it became effortless.

I know a friend that wants to score high on a test. She became fully committed by deleting all her social media accounts for some time. She spent time each day studying for this test. She focused her mind on getting the test score that she wanted. She ended up scoring about 2% over the score that she wished to have. She was very focused, and she concentrated her energy on getting a desirable test result. She took action, and she succeeded.

So for this exercise, I want you to set a goal for yourself that you would like to accomplish in the next three weeks. It doesn't have to be something big. It can be anything like being able to complete a 4-mile run within a certain amount of minutes, writing a short E-book, creating your first blog site, etc. How committed would you be to accomplish this goal? What are you willing to give up to make this goal fruition? Focus your mind on succeeding this goal, be very disciplined, and hold yourself accountable. Take massive action and use repetition to get the result that you want.

Knowing how to do something is good, but repetition is what solidifies findings. I can show you how to ride a bike, but you'll not successfully able to ride a bike until you've practiced doing it a few times. In Adobe Photoshop, when you use the brush tool to paint, you can adjust its opacity. The lower the opacity when you paint, the lighter the color would appear and almost invisible. If you raise the opacity higher, then color would appear solid and visible with just one stroke.

On the other hand, when you lower the opacity. The paint color will appear very light and almost invisible, but if you continue to paint on the same spot over and over, then the color would become robust and more visible. It may seem like you may have a lower opacity in doing things, but trust me, the results are still there. Be patient and be repetitive. Before you set out to do your one big life goal, set out a bunch of small goals and see that you accomplish them; this creates familiarity. It also helps build confidence and also improves your chances of succeeding in your significant goals in life.

Now elite, as you continue to build yourself up. You also want to declutter your mind and your space. Practice being minimalistic. Clean and organize your closet. Take out all the old clothes and shoes that you are no longer using. Give those to somebody else who may need them. If possible, try to limit your clothes and other things to only what you will use. Do not try to be a hoarder. Holding on to too many things that you are not going to use is pointless. It's also a way of telling God, the universe, higher power that you already have enough. If you want to receive, you must be open to it and keep it flowing.

Write down all the things that are going on in your mind. Make time to do all those things and cross out the ones that you are incapable of doing. Learn to let go of the things that you cannot do anything about. Focus on the things that bring you a little bit of happiness. Expand on those things and cherish them.

Remember, Elite, you are your first employer, and you should take yourself very seriously before anyone else will. Before you go out in the real world and take any regular job, you should have mastered yourself physically, mentally, and spiritually. Know your true worth, and do not let someone else figure that out for you. Take on regular jobs as a stepping stone to reach your ideal goals. Do not use your goals as a means of landing a job. Your goals should always be toward your perfect lifestyle. Therefore start re-creating your paradigm to mirror your circle of life.

TAB **2**

Paradigm

A paradigm is just a modeled behavior that everyone else follows—a common example of a Paradigm. In modern Society, People have been accustomed to the idea that they must go to school for some years. After years of schooling, they may get a degree in some fields. They will use that degree to secure a job and work until retirement. This has been the most common Paradigm in our society today. This Paradigm has been passed on to us through our parents, the government, the media, and so forth. The negative effect of this Paradigm is that for one, it has become a sort of a Rat race. It is the main idea that almost everyone is clinching on to for achieving success in society. Another adverse effect of this is that it has caused most people to be genuinely in debt. People took out a tremendous amount of student loans to get a college degree, hoping they'll land a high paying job, but sometimes, it ends up being the opposite. The number of years and money spent getting a college degree doesn't always equate to the salary that they would get after earning that degree. It is not to be negative, but to give you a perspective. Please keep in mind that education is a good thing. You must also understand that most of the things that we do are actions embedded in our minds. You should not feel incompetent in society for not following the same Paradigm as everybody else. There are other avenues in life that you can take to achieve abundance. A lot of times, the things that we do are things that stemmed from a paradigm. Our paradigms are influenced by our parents and society at large. It is kind of why we are mostly all doing the same things. If you have a conversation with another person and ask them who they are, first, the person would tell you their name, and then they would say to you what they do for a living. It is one of the reasons you'll hear some Conspiracy theorists say that people are programmed. The good news is that we can reprogram ourselves. Our brains are considered neuroplasticity. It means that we can rewire our brains and adopt a new way of thinking, thus rebuild ourselves.

Elite start putting fruitful information in your mind. Start changing your Paradigm. Practice doing things differently from usual or try new things. Practice writing with your nondominant hand, take different routes to work. Go out and test drive a Lamborghini or an expensive car that is outside your comfort zone. Fly first class. Eat at a high-end restaurant. Go to a resort, hire a maid for a weekend, give to a charity or your community, find a day to do nothing, feel good about yourself. Etc.

CHECKPOINT 4:
-**Close your eyes and repeat these phrases in your mind:**
 I am powerful!
 I have an abundance!
 I am healthy!
 I am wealthy!
 I feel great!
 I look great!
-**Write these phrases down in your journal**
-**Read these phrases out loud.**
-**Deeply believe in the above statement**

EXERCISE 4
JOURNAL ENTRY

As the powerful human beings that we are, our mind is one of our most powerful assets. We can first create the kind of lifestyle that we want through our minds then cultivate that lifestyle into reality. For this journal entry exercise, start with a rough draft. Brainstorm ideas of the kind of lifestyle that you'll want. Be as selfish as possible and do not limit yourself. After you've brainstormed your ideal lifestyle, next, we will go through the visualization process. Find a quiet, comfortable place. Relax, take a deep breath in, and exhale. Do this at least three times and let go. Let go of any negative thoughts that come into your mind. Close your eyes and see yourself exactly where you want to be about three years from now. Use your imagination and be very detailed. For example, you may want to see yourself in the ideal body that you desire. What does that body look like, as you picture it? See yourself already having the body that you want. How much exactly you would weigh, see the number as you imagine yourself standing on the scale.

Another example is that you may also want to see yourself having the ideal house that you want. Know the exact location where the house would be. How many bedrooms would it have? What color would it be? What type of materials would it be made off? Etc. See yourself as already living in this house, because you are already living in this house. Write about your new home in your journal. Write about it in the present tense, as if you are there now. Write the specific date and time that you see yourself owning this house. For example; Your journal may go something like this: On December 21, 2021, at 2:00 PM, I would be living in Paris close to the beach, in my beautiful four bedrooms, 2bath, glasshouse, …etc. Once you've gotten this journal entry done, read it out loud with a lot of excitement and believe that it would come to be. Read this journal at least twice a day, first thing when you wake up in the morning and last thing before you go to sleep for the next 21 days. Being transparent and specific is how you would start manifesting all your imagination into reality. As I have mentioned before, I believe that it takes at least 21 days to change a habit or develop a new one. Practice the above journal for 21 consecutive days. If you miss a day, start over until you get a full 21 consecutive days. Elite, as you continue this process, you may notice that your mental state would start to change.

TAB 3

Financial thermostat

Everyone has what I called a financial thermostat. Just as the thermostat that controls the temperature in your house to be at certain degrees. A person's commercial thermostat is the amount of money that they may feel like they can attain based on different factors. It can come from how they think about themselves. The amount of education that they may have, the environment that they live or grew up in, and the amount of money that the people closest to them have (parent, friends), etc. A person's financial thermostat is different from the substantial amount of money that they have. A person can have a lot of money physically, but his or her money thermostat could be very low and therefore cause him or her to potentially lose all money earned, either by wasteful spending, giving it away, or somehow incur a situation that would cause unnecessary expenditures. By the way, this is not to say that giving away money is a bad thing. Giving is also receiving, providing if that's your desire. Giving when you are not expecting anything in return is good. When you grant out of kindness, or out of pure passion, it makes you feel good internally and helps you develop an Elite state of mind, and this is what equates giving to receiving.

When a person gives and expects something in return, this means that they haven't entirely given. Another characteristic of People with a low financial thermostat is that they tend to self-sabotage themselves to not having more by feeling unworthy. They may feel incapable of having more, or they may feel like getting more money is just out of their reach. Paradigm can impact a person's Financial thermostat. Other attributes, such as thoughts, feelings, faith, conscious, and subconscious beliefs, contribute to this also. All those factors are interrelated or work side by side with one another. Understanding how to implement these factors can be very beneficial to you. As you read further down, I will give you some of the breakdowns so that you can grasp the concepts better.

TAB **4**

Thoughts

Thoughts are very dynamic. This whole universe was formed from thinking, and we can continue to make it better through our thoughts. If we as human beings collectively start to concentrate our thoughts on the ending of the world, then this would start happening. When we start focusing our thoughts on lack, as if there are not enough resources for every human being, then we will continue to see a decrease. We will start to develop the fear, which could then lead to a hoarding mentality. We will create boundaries among each other to guard our limited resources. We will try to dominate each other's and so forth. Every creation, every invention was first thought of, before it came to be. The clothes that you wear, the food that you eat, the house that you live in right now all came from thinking before it was made to be. Thoughts can change a person's state of being. If you are having funny thoughts in your head, you'll become amused. If you are having angry thoughts, you will start to feel angry. Our thoughts inspire every action we take. Thoughts can control our physical bodies. For example, if you want to go to the Grocery store, you'll first have a view of going to the grocery store before you can physically get up and start going. It would not make sense for you to randomly get up and go to the Grocery store, without any thought of doing so. Thoughts and feelings also work together. For instance, if you are **feeling** sick, you will have **ideas** of going to the Doctor, taking some pills, or lying down. You will end up taking the action of the most dominant thought. This could be either going to the Doctor, taking some medicines or go to lay down. As you've come to understand the power of your thoughts. Start focusing your thoughts only on the things that you want. Pretend that the things that you don't want, don't exist, in other words, concentrate your mind on only your desires.

I'm going to use a biblical reference to illustrate the power of thoughts. It's when Jesus was talking to his disciples. This can be found in the New Testament of the King James Version of Matthew, chapter 5, verse 28. It states, "But I say unto you, That whosoever looketh on to a woman to lust after her hath committed adultery with her already in his heart." That statement is saying that you can commit adultery without any physical contact with the other person. Can you imagine, no physical contact or whatsoever, but Just lusting which comes from our thoughts can be considered adultery. Do not ever underestimate the power of your thoughts." Elite, what kind of ideas do you have today? Are you having positive feelings for yourself and others? Are you having prosperous thoughts or thoughts of misery? Are you having thoughts of wealth or poverty? Are you having thoughts of winning or thoughts of losing? Try to take account of your thinking, and make sure that you are having the thoughts that are going to make your life fruitful.

TAB **5**

Faith

Faith is simply the belief or trust in something not seen in the tangible. Understand that there are three types of "seeing." Seeing in the physical realm (our everyday seeing), seeing in your dreams, and seeing in your imagination. The distinction between these three kinds of seeing is, seeing in the physical domain is something that already exists in our physical plane, or we supposed that already exists. In other words, we may be able to touch it or interact with it. Our minds interpret it as real. Seeing in our dreams is something that is put together by our sub-conscious mind. We have no control over this. We can only do this in our sleep. Seeing in our imagination is something that we consciously create. We do this when we are awake. Seeing in the imagination is where our faith lies. Faith is one of the most omnipotent attributes that can help propel your vision. Another one of my favorite bible phrases, from the King James version: In Matthew Chapter 17, verse 20. It reads: "If ye have faith as a grain of a mustard seed, ye shall say unto this mountains, Remove hence to yonder place; and it shall remove; and nothing shall be impossible unto you." This quote perfectly illustrates the dynamics of having faith. It sometimes takes a lot of confidence for people to develop trust. Some people can base their belief in past experiences, while others found their faith in the feeling of optimism.

There are many ways to illustrate faith, such as You can show faith by uttering your beliefs or by your action. A person can also cultivate faith by having mental images. For example: if you are trying to nurture the trust of having $200,000,000 in your bank account by the year 2025. All you have to do is to continually have a mental image of the $200,000,000 in your bank account. You'll start having the feeling of already having it, and this will help boost your confidence or your faith. Then align your action towards this by investing, seeking other ways to increase your income, and so forth. You can start to develop more trust by holding a physical and or mental image of the thing in which you are trying to cultivate — this idea, also known as a vision board. A Vision Board is a board with printout pictures or magazine cut-out pictures of things that you are trying to accomplish. For instance, if you are trying to have a Lamborghini, a mansion, and $200,000,000 in your bank account, you would get plain board, print our pictures of a Lamborghini, a house, and bundle of money, then paste those pictures onto the board. It would be your vision board. You can also get a blank check and write the amount of $200,000,000 payable to you at a specific date in the future and paste that on your vision board. You can be as creative as you want with your vision board. Once you have all the pictures on the board, you would then place the board where you can see it daily, morning, and night. You would want to make sure it's the first thing you see when you wake up in the morning and the last thing you see before you go to bed at night. You would do this all while at the same time regularly having mental images of the same things in your mind. Doing this can help strengthen your faith also. Vision boards are more advance than a New Year's resolution. Vision boards give you a visual reference point. A New year's resolution, on the other hand, can sometimes be interpreted by the mind as just wishful thinking. A lot of times, when people make a New Year's resolution, they don't already see it into fruition, but they say it to justify their ego or make themselves feel better like they are onto something. The mind can interpret a New Year resolution as just a challenge or a punishment, and therefore makes it harder because you are going against your comfort zone. A vision board is much more subtle, stationary, and yet serves as a constant reminder or motivation. You have an ideal goal in your mind. Creating a vision board is like projecting the ideas in your mind on to a mirror. Being able to see your goals in front of you makes things much more exciting.

CHECKPOINT 5:

-Close your eyes and repeat these phrases in your mind:

    I am powerful!

    I have an abundance!

    I am healthy!

    I am wealthy!

    I feel great!

    I look great!

-Write these phrases down in your journal

-Read these phrases out loud.

-Strongly believe in the above statement!

EXERCISE 5
CREATE

- Create your vision board. Use the information from your journal entry in exercise #4. Create a vision board for the life that you want.

- For the next thirty days, as you continue with exercise #4, try to pay attention to your thoughts. Anytime you notice negative thinking try to discard it and replace it with a positive one. For example, you may be driving to work and start seeing traffic build-up. It could arise to negative thoughts like "I'm going to be late for work." As soon as you notice this thought, quickly re-phrase this thought with a positive one such as "I will make it to my work today on time, no matter what." Use this for any other situation. It helps you to be in control and to navigate your life. It may be challenging at first, but as an Elite, we stay in practice even with the little things, and this is how we get better. You are an Elite!

TAB **6**

Affirmations

Affirmations are like the programming of our conscious and subconscious mind. They are thoughts, experiences, or words that we've accepted to be true, whether consciously and or unconsciously. They are like cassette recording that keeps playing in our minds. Just as thoughts, affirmations also have the power to control the outcomes of our lives. Affirmations can be deliberate. Other times, they are infused onto us by our parents, peers, teachers, co-workers, or the environment. Affirmations can be positive or negative. Here are some examples of affirmations. Let say that you grow up with abusive parents who always told you that you are worthless. Eventually, this may become one of the narratives deep in your subconscious mind and would sometimes keep playing in your head repeatedly, even without you noticing. You would then develop the feeling of worthlessness as time goes on. One of the quickest ways to reverse this is to keep telling yourself that you are worthy of your thoughts and also by voicing it out loud too. This is also where prayer may come in handy. Prayers, in a sense, are like affirmations. When you pray, you are telling yourself the truth. Start using prayer to your advantage. You may also want to listen to positive affirmation recordings over and over to help overcome the negative ones, then start acting as you've affirmed yourself to be. Listening to positive affirmation frequently is like re-writing the negative ones that have been implanted by you or others. As you become more cognoscente of these ideas, you should also physically start implementing them. Elite, at this time, you may have already grabbed the concept. Always try to align your imagination with your physical being. I will bring up this concept again in the upcoming passages, but for now, let me give you another example of a negative affirmation.

If you live in a poor, crime-infested, deteriorated neighborhood, it will impact your ways of thinking and your world view. It would also reflect in your lifestyle or the way you approach things. It could make you prone to crime. Here is how you can change this type of affirmation: See yourself out of that neighborhood through your mind or by having a vision board of the ideal place that you want to see yourself. You could make it a habit to sightsee other areas with more significant potential. Associate yourself with people in a much better neighborhood and always remember that you are an Elite. No matter where you are right now, and whatever situation that you are going through. I promise you that you have greatness within you!! You were meant to prosper.

TAB 7

Gratitude

Gratitude means being thankful and appreciative of the things you've already got, or the things that you are about to receive. Showing or doing is one way to demonstrate gratitude. Here are some examples. If you want to show appreciation for the car that you own, you can say things like, "I am very thankful for my make, model, year, the color car that I own. You can also practice gratitude by taking good care of the car, doing all the maintenance, and up keeping. You can have an appreciation for the things you wish to have by being thankful for them in advance and using the present tense, with a lot of sincerity and faith. Let say that you would like to be a successful CEO in the future. You can demonstrate gratitude for this as if you are already that CEO by saying things like, "I am very thankful for being the CEO of XYZ." Gratitude should not be limited to tangible items. You can also use appreciation for abstract things like peace, wellness, love, freedom, etc.

TAB **8**

Act as if or Simulate

Simulating can help with the manifestation process also. Use your mind to stimulate your end-state desires and act them out in the physical too.

Start acting as if you already have the things that you desire. Act as if you are the person you would like to become. Let say that you desire to be a professional soccer player. Close your eyes and use your imagination. Vision yourself in the boxing ring. Start shadowing boxing in your mind, and hear the crowd cheer for you. Begin practicing boxing in real life with a trainer. Get all your equipment and start developing a good feeling about this.

Do you wish to be a successful businessman or woman? Start seeing yourself as a businessman or woman. Believe that you are that businessman or woman. Start doing the things that a successful businessman or woman does. Organize events and go to meetings with other business people. Start dressing up as a businessman or woman. Create your business card, even if it's just only for your contact information. Contact your local town or county and inquire about starting your own business. Go to events or seminars and Network with like-minded people. One of the best places to network with other people is through websites like www.meetup.com or www.linkedin.com. There are also mobile apps for these sites. "Meetup" is growing very popular. It allows people to create and host events at different venues of their choice either for recreational or for professional. Depending on your location, this may not be available in your country, but you can always start your platform. You can also start a Facebook group to network with other like-minded people.

CHECKPOINT 6:

-Close your eyes and repeat these phrases in your mind:

I am powerful!

I have an abundance!

I am healthy!

I am wealthy!

I feel great!

I look great!

-Write these phrases down in your journal

-Read these phrases out loud.

-Strongly believe in the above statements!

EXERCISE 6
ACTION, JOURNAL ENTRY

- Write down ten positive affirmations for yourself in the present tense and read them out loud at least once a day. Here are some examples:

  I am very healthy,

  I am strong,

  I am confident,

  I can do all things,

  my life is perfect now,

  I am so pleased right now,

  I am an Elite,

  I live peacefully, etc.

  Notice the state of mind that you'll be in, as you continue to indulge yourself in these affirmations

- Write down five things that you've already have, and that you are grateful to have. For instance: "I am thankful for having a place to sleep in XYZ," "I am very happy for my friends and family," "I am thankful for the XYZ car that I drive, and so forth.

- Get a sticky notepad, and write on it three things that you want to believe about yourself. Write those things from the first-person point of view and write them in the present tense. Stick it somewhere in the bathroom mirror, your computer monitor, or a place where you can see it every day, preferably in your car. You don't have to read these out loud every day. Your subconscious mind would pick them up automatically. Here are some lead examples:

"I am my own boss,"
"I am delighted,"
"I am very wealthy,"
"I have an abundance."
"My life is perfect."
"Good things are always coming to me."

- Next, start using the simulating technique. Use your mind to forecast the things that you desired. In your mind, see yourself already having these things. Start taking small actions or steps to make this simulation happen in the physical.

- Download the Meetup app and create an account. Sign up for at least one meetup event with like mind people in your area

Look, Elite, I understand that some of these ideologies may seem very redundant, but this is about your life, and you deserve greatness. Greatness will come to you by doing. You do by taking small steps, and then you continue to build on these small steps. One of my favorite inspired entrepreneurs that I follow is Ed Mylett. He has a quote that says, "Your obsession, becomes your possession." So Elite, become obsessed with your desired lifestyle.

TAB **9**

The sub-conscious and the Conscious mind.

A mind is a powerful tool. It is the first place for all creation. Every invention that we see was first developed in somebody's mind, then into reality. The two main parts of the mind are the conscious and the sub-conscious. The conscious mind operates on logic. For example, you would not touch a hot stove, because you know that logically, you would get burned. Another thing about your conscious mind is that it wants to be in cruise, and it doesn't like being interrupted. It's also where you have all your excuses, or where you make fresh ones. For example, if I were to tell you to start waking up at 3:00 AM. Your conscious mind would front-load a bunch of logical excuses as to why you should not wake up at 3:00 AM. You may start having thoughts like "It's too dark outside at 3:00 AM," "I won't get enough sleep if I wake up at 3:00 AM," "Whatever I can do at 3:00 AM, I can do it the evenings," etc. Sometimes your conscious mind can pull information from your sub-conscious and have you act upon it.

The subconscious mind, on the other hand, does not operate on logic. It does not care if its right or wrong. Instead, it acts like a sponge. It just sucks up everything that you tell it, through repetition, and it held that to be true. It can work directly or indirectly. The subconscious mind does not only get information from the things that we say. It also picks information from our thoughts. It can get information from the images that we see in our surroundings. Have you sometimes notice out of the blue, a song is just stuck in your head, even though the music is not playing (logically) at the present moment? Those are just old music that you've listened to and have meshed through your subconscious mind. Be cognitive of the music to which you are listening. Have you ever also noticed that you were driving your car, and your brain just drifted somewhere else, but you are still in control of the vehicle? That's just your subconscious mind taking over the wheel. The subconscious mind also works like a muscle. You must train it, and feed it as you would your regular muscles. You can instruct your subconscious mind by your thoughts, your imagination, pictures, reading books, listening to audiotapes, motivational speeches, and so forth. The key is to synchronize your conscious mind with your subconscious one. Try to move your conscious mind from neutral to drive and be in control. The other three main factors that can help shift your conscious mind from neutral to drive are pain, pleasure, and emotion. However, your subconscious is more responsive to pain. You are more motivated to do the things that would give you pleasure. You are more inclined to take action when your emotions are involved or if you face an uncomfortable situation. It is why it's good sometimes to embrace your trial and tribulation. The pain and emotions you go through are some of the composites for inspiration.

So Elite, my question to you is: What have you imprinted in your subconscious mind? Maybe you've experienced poverty your whole life. You have too many bills, struggling to make ends meet, experiencing weight problems, haven't found your real love, or just going through some addiction. Whatever the case may be, **I want you to know that you have the power to change all that and turn your life around for the better.**

Take the time to clear your mind. As I have mentioned before, meditation is one of the very effective ways to tune up your intellect. Just find a quiet place to relax. Close your eyes, breathe in and out slowly. Try to quiet your mind and focus all your attention on the present moment. At this point, from everything that you've read so far, you should've gotten the bigger picture. The bigger picture is that you are the center of your reality.

God, the universe, Mohamed, Jesus, or whatever higher power that you believe in, is only here to witness you do it.

You, my friend, are very special! Just think about it. This whole earth was made just for us as human beings to reside in it, and play our part. Look at everything around you. Everything from the daylight, nighttime, plants, etc., were all created as a contributing factor to make you feel comfortable. On top of all that, you have the power to make life even better. You have to come into agreement with this fact, and everything would start to flow. Perhaps this is why most people feel like they don't see the fruition of their prayers. It's because the thing of which they are praying to get, they've already gotten, or they are capable of creating it. In essence, you are not praying or asking for anything. Start being thankful as you pray, instead of just asking. Be grateful with deep faith, and see yourself already having the thing which you were going to pray and or ask. It is knowledge, and understanding is what you are seeking. The knowledge and understanding that you don't need anything else outside of yourself. The knowledge and understanding that you already have everything that you need or you have the power to create that which you desire.

CHECKPOINT 7:

-Close your eyes and repeat these phrases in your mind:

I am powerful!

I have an abundance!

I am healthy!

I am wealthy!

I feel great!

I look great!

-Write these phrases down in your journal

-Read these phrases out loud.

EXERCISE 7
PRACTICE

- Read inspirational quotes every day for the next thirty days.

- Listen to motivational speeches every day for the next thirty days. Here is a list of good motivation speakers that you can find on YouTube: Les Brown, Eric Thomas, Tony Robbins, David Goggins, Chris Gardner, Zig Ziglar, Jim Rohn, and more.

- Listen to positive affirmations every day, even while you sleep. There is plenty of positive affirmations on a variety of different topics, such as wealth, health, abundance, etc..

TAB **10**

Energy

We, as human beings, are also made up of intellectual energy. I call this the YOU in you. Not your body, not your name, not your occupation but the YOU that is within all that. We can create substance when we compressed our thoughts, feelings, emotions, attitudes, and actions onto things. There is negative energy, and then there is also positive energy. Negative energy is reflected when you are feeling bad. Positive energy is when you're feeling good. If you express positive energy onto a particular task, you are more likely to do it with ease, and also be successful and inspired in the process. On the flip side, when you express negative energy onto a particular task, it becomes harder, you'll miss the potential opportunities and lessons in that specific task. You may not complete that task. The good news is that we have the power to reverse our energy from negative to positive. First, we have to become aware of the kind of energy that we put out. Then we'll need to change our thoughts, feelings, emotion, and attitude towards our encounters. Once we do this, our perspective on these encounters would change for the good. If you find yourself in a negative situation, dwelling this fact can only compound that negative effect. You must change your thoughts, feelings, emotions, and attitude about that position to alleviate it. Elite, as I have mentioned this before. I don't know what kind of situation you may be going through right now, but whatever negative situation that you find yourself in right now, know that there are possibilities for a turnaround. Elite, as you continue to understand the impact of energy, please also remember that energy can also affect the psychological state of people, places, things, etc. A person can give off the power of anger if they have evil thoughts, feelings, and emotions about certain things. The person who was once mad can also be happy or vice versa. It's the same person, just their energy changed. You may have noticed a person who is always down and depressed, but then one day, that same person decided to be happy and glowing. You may say to that person, "Something is different about you," "You are like a new person." You see, it's the same person, but they changed their energy. Almost everything that we do is an expression of energy to a certain degree. When we wake up in the morning, we are expressing energy. When we go to work, we are showing energy. Energy can change the psychological state of being. In December, during the month of the Christmas holiday, for example. You'll notice that the mental state of people, place, and things are very different from any other months. People are shopping more, buying gifts and other new things for themselves or their loved ones. Business is doing the most promotions to get more sales. People are traveling and decorating their houses. You get a different vibe during this month, because of the energy that people express onto this month. Businesses use focused energy on the branding of a particular product through advertising, word of mouth, influencers, endorsement, etc.

Have you ever notice some similar products that are being sold for two different prices all because of the two different name brands? One of the brands has more energy focused on it than the other. Remember, energy is driven by our thoughts, emotions, feelings, actions, and attitudes. I saw an experiment on YouTube of a brand new shoe store in California. The store took some shoes from a Payless shoe store that is usually sold for about $40.00 and price them for $600.00. On the open day of the store, customers flocked the store to buy these Payless shoes, which marked for $600.00. The store manager eventually let people know that it was an experiment and gave people their money back. Elite! Do not fall prey for things that are vanity. Try to focus your energy and thoughts on things that'll bring fruition to your life.

MONEY

The idea of money is simply energy. The Fiat notes or the paper form of the currency is the representation of that energy. To earn more money, you must channel your power to the energy field of money. What this means that you should try to focus your mind on wealth or abundance instead of focusing it on poor or lack. You have to become wealthy before you become wealthy. Start developing the feeling of wealth. Think about how you can make yourself prosper and contribute to society. Think about things that you can do to make life better for yourself and others. You will attract money after you've developed a wealth conscious. The paper form of money, the experiences, and material possessions are the physical representation or the expression of the wealth you've created in your mind. Wealth is the desirable inner state of feeling, experience, and expression. Wealth is not something that you can calculate. You can only add up your money and material possession. You don't have to possess a certain amount of money for you to be wealthy, if you think this way, you will never be wealthy. When you are going to a job that you hate, that is not a form of wealth. Do not use words like "I am broke," this will register onto your subconscious and becomes your reality. Remember, your subconscious mind does not filter anything. It believes whatever you tell it, whether good or bad, true or false. It does not try to prove you right or wrong; it just accepts. Do not surround yourself by people with a broke mentality, or it will end up becoming your reality. Energy flows where ever you focus your mind or the environment that you surround yourself in. Another way of viewing this concept is like listening to the radio. If you tune in to 92.9, then you'll experience or hear whatever is playing on that station. If you want to hear or experience something different, you'll have to change the station. Know that the money that you deserve does exist. Start asking yourself the questions like: "how can I attract the money that I want." Doing this puts your mind in a creative perspective, and help it comes off of neutral. This action will also spark your inner motivation to go out and seek answers. There is a biblical reference to this. From the King James Version, in the book of Matthew 7:7-8. It reads "Ask, and it shall be given you; seek, and ye shall find; knock, and it shall be opened unto you: For every one that asketh receiveth; and he that seeketh findeth; and to him that knocketh, it shall be opened. Think of this from a common-sense standpoint. If I were to ask you what is 1+1? You'll then try to come up with the answer. If no one ever asks you what is 1+1? You'll never have thought to just come up with the solution. Our minds always want to be fulfilled, that's why whenever it receives an order or a question, it sparks creativity and motivation. Have you ever tries to recall a memory, but can't seem to produce it? It could be anything, like the name of someone you met, or a particular place that you've visited before. You'll notice that the memory would be in the back of your head, but your mind can't just put it together. It would create some discomfort to your mind. Even if you decide to give up on recalling this memory, your mind will still be searching for the answer sub-consciously. Maybe in a couple of days later, this memory would pop right back in your mind. All of a sudden, you'll have a light bulb moment, and you'll remember the exact name of the person you met or the particular place you've visited and so forth. So Elite, start putting your mind in a very creative space instead of limiting yourself, especially when it comes to money. Money is significant in our society. Almost everything that we do revolves around money. The food that we eat, the clothes that we wear, etc.. These are all monetary by-products. With this in mind, most people try to hold on to cash. Generally, people try to cut back on their expenses to save money. While this idea is beneficial, but it always right to think of ways to expand and flourish instead of trying to be small. Cutting back or denying yourself from self-expression is not an efficient way to become wealthy. Authentic self-expression is true Freedom, and it's true Freedom that the soul is seeking. Another thing that prevents people from attaining the kind of money that they deserve is because sometimes people have a negative resentment towards money. They may want money, but deep in their sub-conscious, they may think of money as evil. Unfortunately, most of the unfortunate events that occur in our society have some monetary association. You may have seen on the news that someone got rob or killed for money. You may have known some people who have done the wrong things for monetary gains. All this builds up a negative perception of money in your subconscious mind, whether you've realized it or not. There is a bible verse from Timothy 6:10 that says, "For the love of money is the root of all evil." This statement also creates a negative perception of money. Out of that entire statement, for some people, their minds would only pick out the word "money," and "evil," then associates the two. Deep in their sub-conscious, when they think of money, they think evil or vice versa. That statement was just a reminder that most evil stems from the love of money. You should never consider this if you are not planning on doing any evil deeds. As part of developing the Elite state of mind, you should always have an ethical mindset. A mind far from evil doings. Think of yourself as having an elevated mindset to bring peace, joy, happiness to yourself, your fellow humans, and the planet. Start building a positive relationship with money. Take good care of your money, the same way you would your car, or your house. In the end, it's not the money that we want, but the Freedom that money would bring us.

CHECKPOINT 8:

-Close your eyes and repeat these phrases in your mind:

I am powerful!

I have an abundance!

I am healthy!

I am wealthy!

I feel great!

I look great!

-Write these phrases down in your journal

-Read these phrases out loud.

EXERCISE 8
JOURNAL

Strengthen your money perspective. Use at least 20 pages in your journal entry. Write the following statements. "I have plenty of money," "money comes to me easily," "money is good." This journal entry doesn't have to get done in one sitting. You can take a couple of days and do this habitually.

TAB **11**

The one-day theory and time

Elite, as you continue to build yourself up, do not be too fixated on time. Time is just an illusion. Time is only an artificial method that people use to measure or reference parts of the day. You may hear people say things like, "I don't have time for this," or "I don't have time for that." Some people may say, "I'm running out of time." These are all perceptions that people create based on the context of time. Elite, I tell you today, you do have time. Go, and do it! Whatever things that you've had wanted to do, but felt like you didn't have that much time to, go start doing those things today. In today's society, people are very time conscious. It is because almost everything that we do is time-based. When you go to your work, your job compensates you for your time. If you want to schedule a doctor's visit or a meeting, you'll schedule them with time. Even though time is just an illusion, and it's not occupying any space or holding any physical capacity. It has become one of the most precious commodities in modern-day society. Some people have even made it a thing to try to figure out how to manage their time. People apply different time management strategies to gain more time. I tell you, Elite, always focus on managing yourself, and everything else will fall into place. You have no control over time, but yourself. You cannot achieve something that you have no control over. Time is linear, and it operates in a continuum. Time holds no physical properties, and therefore you cannot manage it. For example, if it takes you 10 minutes to run from point A to point B. The only way that you can improve the time that it takes for you to get to point B is by training or managing yourself to be faster. You can also train your legs to be much stronger and doing cardio exercises.

Elite, another shifting perspective that I want to introduce you to is based on the days of the week and the weekends. As you are going through this process of shifting your paradigm, you should know that there is only one day of the week, and that is today. Yesterday was today, tomorrow will be today and today is today. Do not become too personal with the day by considering it with several different names, such as Monday, Tuesday, Wednesday, Thursday, etc. Every day is the same, but it just the energy that people have placed on the day that makes it what it is, in perception. For example, most people hate Mondays because it is the first day of the week and they have to start work. People look forward to Fridays because it's the last day of the weekdays and the final workday for most people. You may have heard people saying the phrase "Thank God It's Friday," or TGIF. It's phrases like these that shows people's attitude for that particular day. There is a restaurant chain named TGIF founded in the United States. Fridays and especially the weekends are when people do most of their traveling, partying, outing, shopping, etc. It's all people's feelings, thoughts, and energy that is centered around those particular days that make them what they are. Elite, in the next six months or so, as you continue to work your first job or to build yourself up. Please understand and follow these fundamental principles that I have outlined in this book. I challenge you for the next six months to try to reverse all the paradigm that has been set forth by society and see how your perspective will start to change.

While you are working your first job, your new slogan should be TGIE, which means Thank God It's Everyday! Start treating every day as the same. Wake up on the weekends, the same time that you usually wakes up during the weekdays. Do not look at the weekends as the time to just party or lazing around. Use these days to do your journaling, researching ideas, meditating, and reflecting on yourself. Please note that I am not referring you to be Workaholic, but instead, you are retraining and building up your perspective and shifting your paradigm. Society has conditioned people. Most people do the same things Monday through Friday. They most likely wake up around the same time every day of the week, do their hygiene, drive the same route to work, and most likely stop by the same fast-food restaurant to grab breakfast. It's kind of like a fence is placed in our minds, and we can only do things within that fence. It gets uncomfortable each time that we try to go outside of this fence. Elite, your goal is to destroy that fence completely or push it further, so that you can have a more significant land, to honestly and freely express yourself.

TAB **12**

What is your Why?

You may have heard a lot of motivational speakers and entrepreneurs talk about their "why" statement. A "Why" statement pretty much answers the question of why do you want to do the things that you want to do. Why do you want to be successful? Understanding the response to the question could be the dynamic force that is going to push you through. The bigger your "why" is, the more likely you are to push through any opposition that you may face. When your "why" is more significant than your excuses, then all your obstacles would become smaller. Your "why" is something that is pressing you to want to succeed in life. It could be because you want your daughter or son to live the life that you never lived. Perhaps your "why" is because someone else life is dependent on you. Maybe your "why" is because you are tired of living a mediocre lifestyle. When your "why" is so strong that you may be knocked down ten times and still able to get up. When I first started writing my original book, I joined a book club. I met some terrific people at my book club. I've learned a lot from them. Every other week at the Book Club, we would all submit a couple of pages from our rough draft to be critiqued by each other. I remembered one day I showed up to the Book Club without my rough draft because I had been very busy at work. I let the members know that I wasn't able to write anything for those past two weeks. Every member seemed to understand my situation, except for this one older man. The old man pulled me to the side and asked me: "You didn't submit your rough draft for this week?" I looked at him and replied: "No." The old man got up and looked at me very fiercely and said: "Why not?" and continued to stare at me as I was getting ready to reply to him. From the look on his face, I knew that no matter what kind of ration-able explanation that I would've tried to come up with, it would've seemed like I was only making excuses. Instead, I looked at him and said: "You right! Really why not?" We both looked at each other and burst out laughing. He was such a jokester, but he always motivated me. At times, he approaches me so very strongly, and I can't tell if he is joking or not. The day that he asked me the "why not," question was the day that I thought to reconsider my "why" statement—every time I set goals for myself, no matter how big. At the end of it, I always ask myself the question "Why not?" knowing that no matter what rational explanation that I would try to come up with, it would just sound like an excuse. So Elite, today I ask you, why not? Maybe you are thinking of having $200,000,000 in your bank account within the next six years. Why not? You may be thinking of owning your own private jet in the future. Why not? Dream big, Elite! Don't ever limit yourself.

CHECKPOINT 9:

-**Close your eyes and repeat these phrases in your mind:**
   I am powerful!
   I have an abundance!
   I am healthy!
   I am wealthy!
   I feel great!
   I look great!
-**Write these phrases down in your journal**
-**Read these phrases out loud.**

EXERCISE 9
JOURNAL CREATE YOUR WHY STATEMENT

Refer back to your Exercise 4 and 5, the ideal lifestyle that you've already created. What is your "Why" statement for creating this lifestyle? Why should you deserve this kind of lifestyle? What are your deserving factors? Are you willing to work hard? Are you ready to overcome any obstacles that you may face? This idea goes back to prayer or having gratitude for something. If you are going to pray and ask for something, make sure that you've done all that you could to deserve it before showing gratitude or praying for it. Do not be lazy and expect miracles to happen. Play your part Elite. For example, if you are going to pray for good health, then ask yourself what have you done to have good health. Have you been exercising? Have you been eating healthy? etc

TAB **13**

Action

Action is one of the most crucial elements that would get you to your point B. Start taking purpose-driven action to reach your destiny. Our thoughts, energy, beliefs, and even our paradigm are what helps to fuel the action that we take. Sometimes, also just spending some money to buy the course, the coaching program, the self-help book could be one small action that'll bring you closer to your destiny. One of my favorite lines from successful speaker Tony Robins is that "progress equals happiness." One of the main reasons why most people would stop taking action towards their goal is because they stop seeing progress. Whenever you are trying to succeed at anything, the moment that you start seeing growth, this will create momentum, and it'll increase your motivation to keep going. Action is the catalyst for progress; progress leads to success, and success creates momentum. There are two types of momentum; stored momentum and streaming momentum. The more success one gets the more action that they'll take to keep getting more success or duplicate their success.

There are two types of success; gradual and instantaneous. Incremental success is small, and it's occurring. Instantaneous success can happen almost instantly. I call this the success cycle, with its four key components being action, progress, success, and momentum. This cycle would be less functional if one of its key elements is missing.

When you first approach a goal or a project, you have stored momentum. It is when the vision or ideas are just in your mind, and you are getting ready to take action. You are not likely to take action without any stored momentum unless you already have some streaming momentum. Streaming momentum occurs after you start achieving success. It allows you to keep going and taking more action. You may not reach success without progress. Progress provides you feedback. When you first start working on a goal, your first objective is to see some progress, and this tells you that you are on the right track. Progress can be time-dependent or action dependent. It may sometimes take a very long time for one to start seeing progress. Other times, one may need to increase their action to start seeing progress. Without success, there may not be any momentum. Without any momentum, one may not take any action.

Action is a very vital instrument. You can have thoughts of achieving something, but it would be pointless if you don't take any action towards it. It is a good thing to have a New year's resolutions. It is good to create a vision board. It is good to have a positive mindset, and so on, but unless you take a course of action, everything else would just be good potential. The action occurs when you are moving, when you start making the calls. When you start writing your goals down, go to the seminars, watching motivational speeches, buying the self-help books, and read them. The action occurs when you purchase online coaching courses and do them. When you go to networking events, it occurs when you start doing the research, etc. These are all actions that you can take, so begin taking massive actions today!.

TAB 14

Our Belief System

Elite as you continue to read some of these ideas, they may sound too simple to be true and therefore make it very difficult to believe. You may still be having doubts that you are capable, that you can overcome, that you have the power inside of you. One of the reasons why you may still be having doubts is because of your belief system. You see, Elite, as human beings, our belief system comes standard with our five basic senses. Our sense of touching, seeing, hearing, smelling, and tasting. For most people, they solely rely on these five senses to have a strong belief in something. If they come across a thing or a situation where they can't see, touch, feel smell, or taste, then they most likely would not have a strong belief in that thing or situation. Elite, even though you may not be able to touch, hear, taste, smell or see it for yourself right now but I still want you to know that you can reach your dreams and do the things that you've always wanted. Therefore I encourage you to use these other instruments that I have already mentioned before as part of your belief system. Use Faith, imagination, and thoughts. Always know that just those three instruments are more potent than your five senses. To put this in a quantifiable perspective, see the table down below.

TYPE OF SENSES	PERCENTAGE OF BELIEVENESS
SEEING	15%
TOUCHING	15%
HEARING	15%
SMELLING	15%
TASTING	15%
FEELING	15%
EXPERIENCING	10%

I considered Feeling and Experience as also another form of sense. From the chart above, each one of our senses (seeing, touching, hearing, smelling, tasting, feeling) is 15% of our belief. Except for experience, which is the most abstract, and it only counts for 10% of our belief system. For example, if you can see and touch something, but you can't hear it, smell it, taste it, experience it, or feel it, then your belief in that thing or situation is only at 30%. Another attributes that can factor our belief system is our thought and faith. Thoughts alone are 80% of our belief system, while faith by itself is

60% of our belief system. Our thoughts are the most powerful because you can use your thoughts to cultivate the other senses. With enough concentrated thought also, a person can start developing faith. For most people, whenever they come across something that they have not expressed much thoughts and faith in, or if it is beyond their five senses, they think that it doesn't exist, or they wouldn't believe in it. For most people, it harder for them to comprehend or believe in something that is outside of their five senses. On another subject, I feel like perhaps this is one of the main reasons why some people don't believe in God or a higher power. I feel like God's dynamic is so far beyond our five senses that it can be hard to somethimes grasp with our level of understanding, and thus very hard to believe. Elite, I'm saying all these to say that you must express concentered thoughts and faith along with your five senses for the things that you want.

TAB **15**

Problems or Trial and Tribulation

Elite, there are no problems. There are only situations. Anytime you are faced with a position, it would continue to be a situation until you decide what kind of interpretation that you are going to give it. For example, you may have some bills due, then all of a sudden you lost your job. That incident has now created a situation. You may interpret this situation as the end of your life. You are going to be homeless and so forth. Those sets of thinking could cause the condition to cripple you. The more you dwell on the negative aspect of the situation, the more it would become a problem in your mind. You will miss out on the lesson, the opportunity that the case was trying to present to you. Another way that you can view this kind of situation is that it's the beginning of a whole new life — the birth of a new chapter. Your so-called problems are only more significant when they are just floating in your head. They will continue to be this gigantic super villain that always causes you stress. Elite, be the superhero. You invariably want to write down all your problems on a piece of paper so you can look down on them as the giant that you are!. After you have done the extraction process. Beside each problem, write down what kind of solution or what action you are going to take to close out these problems. For the ones that you cannot come up with a solution, just let them go and move past them. Your primary focus should be the solution for these so-called problems, and not the issues themselves.

Whenever you encounter a situation or a perceived problem, the questions that you want to ask yourself are as follows: What does this situation mean? What lessons is this situation trying to teach me? Who do I need to become for this situation? What opportunities are in this situation? How can I grow from this situation? Always remember that things are happening for you, not to you. Sometimes you need pain or problem to serve as fuel to get to where we want to go in life. It was the problem of being too hot or too cold that ultimately led to the invention of the air conditioner. Challenges are there to remind you of where you don't want to be, the things you don't want to experience. Elite, your problems are not big. You have to become bigger!

TAB **16**

Find Inspiration

No matter what you are going through, there other people who have had it worse than you. Elite, make it a habit at least once a week to read up on short biography on successful people who've had to overcome obstacles. Doing this will change the way you view your problems, and it would also give you the courage to push through. Take people like Oprah Winfrey, who had a challenging childhood. She grew up in poverty. At some point in her life, she had to dress up in potato sacks because she couldn't afford regular clothes. At around the age of 9, some of her relatives sexually abused her. By the age of 14, she became pregnant but lost her baby. At the age of 19, Oprah began co-anchoring the local evening news in Nashville, Tennessee. Oprah's big break came in around 1983 when she started hosting the Chicago's WLS-TV low rated half-hour morning talk show "AM Chicago." Within months after Oprah took over, the show became the highest-rated talk show in Chicago. About three years later, the show segment expanded, and they renamed it the "Oprah Winfrey Show." To this day, Oprah has become a well-known celebrity. She has impacted and inspired a lot of people throughout the world. Oprah has considered to be one of the richest black woman in the US.

People like Christopher Gardner. He grew up without any male role model. Chris was placed in foster care while his mother was in Jail. After high school, Chris enlisted in the US Navy. After he got out of the navy, Chris faced some uphill battles. He was arrested and charged with parking tickets fines, and he also became homeless. Chris had to sleep in public bathrooms, parks, church shelters to survive with his son. All this was happening while he was working as a trainee with no pay at a stock brokerage firm. Despite all the adversity that he had to face, Chris thrived at his job. He was good at selling stocks. At the end of his trainee program, they made him a full-time employee with pay. Christopher was then able to rent a home for himself and his son. His career suddenly started to grow, and his whole life changed. In 1987 he opened up his investment called Gardner Rich. The movie "The Pursuit of Happyness," starring Will Smith Was about Christopher Gardener's life. Today Christopher travels around the world to do some motivational speaking to inspire other people.

People like Curtis Jackson, also known as "50 Cent." 50 cent grew up in South Side Jamaica Queens, New York. His mom was killed mysteriously at the age of 8. At around the age of 12, 50 Cent started dealing drugs and eventually dropped out of school. At around the age of 19, the police arrested him for Drugs. 50 Cent later started pursuing his career in music. Upon the release of his first album entitled "The Power of Dollar." 50 Cent was shot multiple times. 50 Cent survived those gunshots, and he came back and started making more mixtapes. Marshall Mathers, also known as "Eminem discovered 50 Cent. "Around 2003, 50 Cent released his debut album titled "Get Rich or Die Trying." With the title of that album, and the dynamic content that it contained plus the person that 50 Cent was, made that album an instant classic for all hip hop fans. That album went to sell well over nine million copies. Today 50 Cent has continued to receive commercial success from Video Games, books, movies, TV Shows, and much more. Elite, there are countless stories like these that you can read about to gain inspiration and courage. What is your narrative? Who are you going to inspire? Are you going to let pain stop you? Remember Elite, that pain produces power. Own your discomfort and use it as an anchor!

CHECKPOINT 10:

-**Close your eyes and repeat these phrases in your mind:**

I am powerful!

I have an abundance!

I am healthy!

I am wealthy!

I feel great!

I look great!

-**Write these phrases down in your journal**

-**Read these phrases out loud.**

EXERCISE 10
FIND YOUR INSPIRATIONS

For the next 60 days, each week, find at least one person that inspires you then read about their life story. It doesn't have to be somebody super famous. Here are some examples. Billionaire PA, who went from selling dope, being in and out of jail over 15 times, to becoming a CEO. Richard Montanez, the janitor who discovered the Flaming hot Cheetos. Dean Graziosi, Manny Khosbin, Brian Dulaney, Tom Bilyeu, Gerrain Jones, Omar Elattar, Chris Cavallini (he got arrested about 17 times, and now he is a CEO of $10 Million company).

Elite, as you can see, no matter where you are in life, no matter what situation you are going through, other people are going through a similar situation or perhaps worse than you. You may feel like you are alone in the dark. You may feel like all the doors have been close down on you. You may feel like you've reached a dead-end. No matter what, you have the power to turn your life around. Decide now that you are going to do this.

TAB **17**

The Elite Laws

Here are some laws that you can utilize to pivot your life or take to your advantage. The first law is the law of attraction: The law of attraction states that you attracted what you are. This idea means that if you are always focusing on the negative, then you'll continue to see or experience negative results. It is why it's good advice to always focus on only the things that you want. Pretend that the things you do not wish do not exist. For example, if you're going to be healthy, focus your thoughts on being healthy. Do the things that healthy people would do, like maintaining a proper diet and exercising. Do not focus on sickness. Only focus on the result of the things that you want. Elite, think of yourself as a magnet. All your thoughts, the things that you say, or hear can drastically impact your life. Always try to think positive thoughts, say positive things, and listen to positive messages, then you'll continue to see positive results. Remember Elite; words have power too. This whole world was spoken into existence by God. Your life would be a reflection of the things that you say or hear. So Elite, what are you speaking of or hearing today? Are you speaking of positive things for yourself and others around you? Are you in an environment where you hear a lot of negativity? Change that environment! The law of attraction also goes for reading and writing as well. Do not continuously read about negative news or gossip celebrity tabloids. You can make the law of attraction work for you by focusing your thoughts and energy with deep emotion on only the things that you want. Imagine this whole world is a blank canvas, and you are an artist. What are you going to paint in it?

The next law is the law of repetition: The law of repetition is as simple as it sounds. If you keep repeating the same thing over and over, then you'll start to believe in it. This law ties back to the law of attraction. You can apply the law of repetition to the law of attraction to have a much more powerful outcome.

Another law that I want to talk about is the law of reciprocity: This is when someone does something beautiful for you, you will feel deeply compelled to want to do something superb in return for them. This law is very vital, and it can also be looked at from a different angle or reinstated as giving to receive or giving equals to receiving. Elite, if you want good things to happen to you, then it must come from within you first. What are you giving out to the world, to the people around you and yourself? Giving is not only limited to tangible gifts. It could be anything like providing useful advice, praying, forgiving, sending out positive messages, and so on. Most people think that giving is only benefiting the person who is receiving, but I'm here to tell you that it goes both ways. This same thing goes for forgiving. Elite any time you give or forgive another person, this would only make you feel good internally. Here is a paraphrased quote from Nelson Mandela on this subject "Resentment is like drinking poison and hoping that it will kill your enemy. Whenever you are holding resentment against someone else, you are doing more harm to yourself than the other person. Holding something back from someone is the same as depriving yourself.

CHECKPOINT 11:
-Close your eyes and repeat these phrases in your mind:
    I am powerful!
    I have an abundance!
    I am healthy!
    I am wealthy!
    I feel great!
    I look great!
-Write these phrases down in your journal
-Read these phrases out loud.

EXERCISE 11
REACH OUT!

Elite for this exercise, I want you to go out and reach out to people. Look up some of your old friends and relatives. Reach out to them to see how they are doing. Elite, spread the love, and it will return to you in greater abundance. If you are looking to be more structured or have consistency, you should have a designated day or a time in the day that is allocated to spread blessing to others.

Here is another law, and it's called the law of averages: Some people sometimes view this law as a fallacy, but as an Elite, you should see this law as taking massive action. The law of averages is the idea that if you are aiming to hit a target, instead of just taking one single shot towards that target. You must make a bunch of multiple shots at the objective, which increases your chance or probability of hitting it or come very close to it. This law help, especially if you are trying to become an entrepreneur, which we are going to discuss further down in this book. One of the many things that cause most entrepreneurs to fail is that they only make one attempt or use one perspective to reach their goals. Its sometimes a good idea to try from multiple different angles, different perspectives, and numerous various attempts

TAB **18**

The World is just like a computer

Imagine when you first bought your computer. With all the necessary software installed, it allows you to be able to paint, create a word document, PowerPoint presentation, and so forth. There is even more advanced software that can enable people to create an animation video, graphic designs, movies, etc. Some of that software already comes with pre-made templates that people can use as an example or a guide. The creator of the computer gives it the possibility to do these things. Each time a person creates something with the computer, whether it's computer animation movies, video games, writing a book, etc. The maker of the equipment does not come forth to help that person create those things. It is up to the creative mind of the person who is using the machine to tap into the creating possibilities of the device, and use it to create what he or she imagined or intended. This concept is also true for the world that we live in right now. With all the resources that are available to humankind, the creator of this world already made it possible for humanity to be able to create. There are endless possibilities. It is up to us as humans to use our creative minds and tap into the innovative nature of the world and design the kind of life that we desire. The world that we live in wasn't physically constructed. Instead, it came into existence through a combination of pre-thoughts, intention, knowledge, imagination, all in an endless spiral of possibilities. It is up to us as humans to tap into this higher potential. There would never be a day when humans will find all there is to discover, create all there is to be created. Know all there is to know because this will then make us God.

TAB **19**

Debts

Elite, there are two kinds of debts. There is "progressive debt," and there is regressive debt. "Progressive debt" is a type of debt that you get into with the potential of compounding your income or growing your income. For example, if you loan money from the bank, to start your own business, this is "progressive debt" because your business could potentially make you more money. Whenever you use debt as an instrument to bring forth more income, it's known as Progressive debt. Of course, you want to take your time and do a lot of planning and research before you get into any progressive debt. Regressive debt, on the other hand, is a type of debt that you get into without the potential of bringing you any money back. These are things such as payday loan, credit card loan, house mortgage, etc. You want to try to avoid regressive debt as much as possible, or any liability for that matter. Debt, especially regressive debt, not only impact your bank account, but it can also affect your wealth and well-being. Having regressive debts can cause a lot of stress and anxiety. It can also limit you from doing the things that you want to do. Having no obligation is the first step to creating wealth and financial freedom. Here is a method that you can use to go about eliminating your regressive debts. First, write down all your debts, then write down the minimum monthly payment for each one of your regressive debt from smallest to highest. Next, you are going to multiply your minimum monthly payment by 2, then add it up with the rest of your other minimum monthly payment. The total of this amount will be your regressive debt payment allocation amount for each month. You should have a separate account that is designated only for regressive debt payment.

From a mathematical perspective, that equation will look like $2X+X+X+X=RDPAA$ (Regressive debt payment allocation amount). The X will represent your minimum monthly payment for each one of your regressive debt. You may have more or fewer X's, depending on your regressive debts. It means that you are going to pay twice the minimum payment for your smallest regressive debt each month. Once your smallest debt is paid up, use that money towards your next smallest regressive debt. You will keep repeating this process until all your regressive debts are paid off. For example, let's say you have three different regressive obligations with a minimum payment of $5, $10, and $15. Your equation will be $2(5)+10+15=35$. So your RDPAA for this example is $35. What this means that you'll keep paying $10 (double the minimum) for your smallest debt, the minimum of $10 for your middle deficit, and the minimum of $15 of your next debt, which adds up to a monthly payment of $35. You'll keep doing this until your lowest debt is paid off, then move that (double minimum payment amount) of your smallest debt towards your next deficit. In this example, you will be paying $20 minimum, instead of $10 towards your consequent debt, while this is just a suggestion. You can also multiply your lowest minimum monthly payment by three or $3X+X+X$, depending on the amount of money you will be able to allocate for your debt. The goal is to be bold with your regressive debt. Be aggressive with regressive. Elite, you may have to get a second job if that what it takes to get rid of all your regressive debts.

TAB 20

The Power of Asking

Elite, you may recall from earlier passages where I talked about the subject of asking. I want to illustrate another point on asking. Asking stems creativity. Even when you are in a difficult situation, asking how you can see yourself out of it can be one of the steps to overcome that particular situation. Asking brings your thoughts and focus together, and thus sparks creativity. Imagine a Company meeting where the boss is outlining all the problems of the company, then immediately skips to the next subject and start talking about other plans until the session ends. Even though members in that meeting understood and acknowledge the problems that the boss mentioned in that meeting, they would not be very eager to come up with solutions for those problems. Imagine in that same Company meeting, where the boss outline all the issues of the company, then ask questions like: "How are we going to come up with solutions for these issues?" "What are we going to do to solve these problems or issues?" Asking these questions will put every employee's mind in a creative space, and it would force them to brainstorm and come up with ideas or answers. You see, Elite, the solutions to most of your perceived problems, if not all, do exist. As silly as this may sound, but one of the ways you go about solving your problems is by asking. You've done this before, unconsciously. Now imagine doing this ingeniously with all your problems. Asking can be done in a prayer format or a meditative state. Start right now. Find a quiet place and think of all the things that have been bothering you. Ask yourself how you can go about solving those things. Become in tune with your mind and write down whatever solution that comes forth.

Journal Entry

Elite, today, I want you to think of where your life is right now. Think of your creator, think of the Universe. Examine your current situation right now. Ask yourself this question, or ask your creator, ask the Universe this question. Are you living your most authentic purpose? Is this all that your life was meant to be? Are you living your very best life? If your answer is yes, and you genuinely believe that, then continue to live this way. But if the answer is no, then by any reasonable means, you should do all that you can to achieve your sould desired purpose. This is what life is about.

TAB 21

Focus on Expansion

Elite, as I have mentioned before, money is an essential commodity in Society. We need money for almost all our day to day activities and our survivability. It's because of this that we've been taught both consciously and unconsciously to be very frugal with money. It is also why most people only pay just the minimum of their regressive debt. Their primary focus is "how can I not lose," instead of "how can I win bigger? Elite, saving money is good, but your primary focus should be on how you can expand. When I first started doing my E-commerce business, my main focus was on not losing my money. It wasn't until I went back and re-looked at some of my business transactions, then I realized that I missed out on some great opportunities because I was so focused on not losing my money. When I decided to shift my focus from the mental state of not loosing to the expansion mindset, then I began to see some outstanding returns. Elite, I am not telling to go out and splurge all your money. What I'm saying is that if you have dreams and goals, but your focus is only on not trying to lose your money, then it is like walking in reverse to your dream. This is why it is very important to not have any regressive debts. It would be best if you considered automating all your regressive bills. Elite, you'll start to notice that your mind would become very resourceful as you continue to ask yourself questions such as "How can I be me more?" "How can I have more?" "Why not me?" Elite, I am not telling you to be greedy or be jealous of others. What I am telling you is that you should not focus your mind on lack but gains. Remember that you are meant to flourish and live abundantly. Elite, look around you. Look at all the plants, water, the atmosphere. These were all meant to serve you. **You have to come into the realization that you were meant to be abundance and expand on this idea. Do not just settle for where Society has placed you.**

TAB 22

Be above average

Elite, always try to be above average or above ordinary in any situation. Anytime you are faced with a situation, ask yourself, "How can I be above average?" It is not to say that being average is necessarily a bad thing. As an elite, you always want to raise the bar higher, especially when it comes to achieving your goals. For example, ordinary people only pay their minimum monthly credit card bills. Try to pay up two or more times your minimum credit card payment. I don't know what your financial situation is during the time you are reading this book. You may be thinking you can't afford to make these kinds of payment, but this exactly where the conversation starts, and the mind-shifting begins. Instead of saying to yourself, "I can't," you should think, "how can I afford this." Asking the question "how can I?" set the mind in a creative mode or a searching mode. The word can't is conclusive, and it weakens your mind not to try to look any further. Try to avoid using the "can't" word as much as possible. Average people start their days around 8:00 or do so only because of their jobs. Elite, make it a habit to start your day earlier than usual. Remember, Elite, always go to work on yourself first before working for anybody else, whether through motivationally, physically, or spiritually. For example, if you have to go work at 9 AM, then wake up maybe at 6 AM to own the day. Use that time to do some physical exercises, meditate, or working to become a boss for yourself.

TAB **23**

Your Haters are Your Angels

Have you ever get down your knees and ask God for a miracle or ask him to send you some of his angels to come down and help you with whatever situation that you may be facing? But instead, you find yourself surrounded by a bunch of toxic people, who will go all out to bring you down. These people will try to step on you even when you are already down. People who will smile in your face and gossip behind your back. Yeah, those people! Those people who'll make themselves so important, while making you feel like you are just worthless. People, that are so negative that you start to ask yourself, "How did I end up with these people?" Elite, these are haters. These people feed on the downfall of others.

It took a while for me to understand this concept of forgiving the people who've done me wrong. It was just insane to think about the same people whom I've shown some kindness to are the same ones that would say bad things about me or try to bring me down. In the book "Conversation with God," Neale Donald Walsh used a metaphor to describe how the light felt when God made it. The light didn't know itself to be the light until God had to create darkness. It was only when there was darkness then the light got to experience itself as the light, it got to see its powers, its brightness.

Elite! You are the light! Continue to forgive the people that have done you wrong. Look past them, for they do not know better. Be the light to those people. It is not to justify the wrongdoing of these people. Instead, you forgive them not for them, but yourself. If you continue to hold on to resentment, it would absorb all your light and dim away your radiance. Elite! Remember that Nelson Mandela quote that went something like this. "Resentment is like drinking poison and expecting the other person to die."

As bad as this may sound, but sometimes you need those unfair people for you to thrive to your greatness. Those unreasonable people, those toxic people, are your angels. Being in the military, I've suffered so many depression and anxieties from having to deal with hypocritical and very unbiased people. Having to go through this had forced me to pray harder and to try to better myself. In the past, I've always been going with the flow. I thought to myself that I had a secured job, and everything was okay. It wasn't until I started encountering these unbiased people that I began to start thinking more outside the box, so to speak. I started seeing things from a different perspective. I started realizing all the possibilities and my higher potentials. As I continued to better myself, I watch these people being stuck in that box mentality, working very hard to get promoted, climbing one step in the pyramid to realize that they are even more unfulfilled. I see some of them being brainwashed to believe that they are the biggest and badest, but yet they are just like everyone else. Elite! Always know your true worth, and this has to be defined by you.

Let's go back to the main point. The reason why you may feel like you've never received that miracle you've asked from God is because you have an embedded story in your mind of what a miracle is supposed to be. You may have imagined that a miracle is a bunch of angels coming down from the sky, soaring to your rescue, but instead, God sent you some haters. Elite know that your haters are strategically placed in your life for you to see yourself as the light. Be careful about how you curse your haters because these people are your angels. Use them as motivation to push forward in life. Use them as a deflection!

TAB 24

Your Relationship With God or High Power

Elite! As you continue to embody your true greatness and empowering yourself. Know that is there is another dynamic that is far greater than you. That dynamic is God. Elite, I encourage you to develop a good relationship with God or higher power. Most people view their relationship with God as a one-way street. They think that God is just this powerful figure who only wants people to worship him. While indeed, it is necessary to serve God or higher power. Elite, you seeking God or a higher power is for your own good, and not the other way around. You go to God to find wisdom, to discover your true perfect self. Elite, you need God more than he needs you. See God as a doctor who is going to take away your pain and heals you, when you are indeed in alignment with God or higher power. You'll start to experience your real purpose in life.

THIS IS A TURNING POINT

Elite at this stage, you should have developed an Elite State of mind. From all the exercises and the foundational principles that we've talked about, this should have given you a deeper level of understanding of what it takes to develop an Elite state of mind. To have a more solid foundation, I encourage you to back and reread that chapter and do all those exercises. Maybe give it a day or two then come back to it. Remember Elite; you are not reading this book only to say, "I've read that book." Instead, you are going to use this as a tool or a guide. You will use it to achieve the lifestyle that you truly desire and deserve. This book is for you, Elite!! If you feel like you are ready to move on to the next chapter, then here it goes. The following section is going to cover the entrepreneurial aspect of an Elite professional. The first chapter was to build you up so that you can have what it takes to create your circle of life and to have an inner understanding of the power within. The next section is going to cover some of the tools and strategies as an Elite professional that you can use to get you to your circle of life. So without further due.

CHAPTER 2

START YOUR OWN BUSINESS

One of the quickest ways to become financially free is to start a business or become an entrepreneur. In simplicity, a business is an organization or an economic system where goods, services or ideas are traded for one another or for money. Business can be conducted by an individual or a group of people. The platform to do business can be physical, digital a combination of both. Business is also an investment. It is where assets are allocated to make a profit over time. In today's society, thanks to the help of the internet, anyone, at any location, can virtually start their own business. It is one of the things that drive the economy. It creates opportunities for people. If you are just an employee, you are practically are already in business to a certain degree. Whether you work in a corporation, a Retail store, or a Fast Food Restaurant, you are participating in business to some degree. Most people aren't aware of this. If you have a job, the place that you work at was established by one person or a collective group of people to make a profit. You being an employee, is helping to carry that mission forward, and this essentially makes you a business person, just at the lowest level. It is not to say that being an employee is a bad thing. You should only be an employee if you are doing a job that you are genuinely passionate about. Working at a job should only serve as a means of getting to your point B or your COL.

The main objective of almost every business is to make a profit. Profit is the total gain from the transaction after you deduct your original investment. In order words, it is the difference from your invested amount from the overall outcome. For example, if a person spends $100,000,000 to start a Super Fancy High-end Childcare Business. The $100,000, 000 includes building fees, utilities, equipment, obtaining licenses, hiring employees, etc. Let say; that the same business makes a total revenue of $150,000,000 within a month. The overall profit of that business for that month is the total revenue ($150,000,000) minus the starting capital of ($100,000,000), which makes it a $50,000,000 profit for that month. Even though the primary goal of a business is to make a profit, sometimes it can result in a loss. A loss is when the total revenue is less than the starting capital. In the Child-care business example above, If the total revenue for that particular month would have been $50,000,000, then the total loss for that month would have been the $50,000,000.

Starting a business can sometimes be very overwhelming, especially when it comes to all the legal necessities to structure your activity. Considering this is why it is a good practice to hire an attorney who can help navigate with all the legal aspects. Essential things to know when starting a business. First of all, you must know the different types of businesses there are. There are three main types of businesses, which are: Service, Merchandise, and Manufacturing.

The service business does not offer any physical or tangible products. Its main goal is to provide service for individuals or other companies. Examples are consultation and delivery. Merchandise Business sells products. It can sometimes get its merchandise from a manufacturer at the wholesale price and re-sell them at the retail price. Some examples of Merchandise businesses are Walmart, JC Penny, Target, Lowes, Home Depot, etc. Manufacturing business manufactures or make finished goods, a product from scratch, usually from raw materials and sell them as merchandise. They can sometimes sell those finished products to other manufacturing companies, who will then use that finished product to make a much more complex product. Example of a manufacturing business is General Motor Corporations (GMC), General Electric, Boeing, etc.

Forms of Business

There are different types of businesses, such as Sole proprietorship, Partnership, Corporation, and limited liability companies. A Sole Proprietorship is owned and operated by an individual. A partnership is a type of business that is carried by two or more individuals. They combine their assets, skills, and labor for the company, and they share the profit and losses of the business equally. A corporation is a business entity that is formed by a group of people. A corporation is a separate body on its own. The identity of a corporation is distinct from its owners. Limited Liability Company, or LLC for short, is a form of business that kind of put a curtain over its members. It helps them hide their identities. The liability or the profit and losses do not extend beyond the business. The members of a Limited Liability Company are sometimes called Shareholders. The burden, contributions, or other rights of people in an LLCs are based on how many shares they have in the company. Now that you have gotten a basic understanding of the different types of business that there are. Our primary focus is going to be doing business as a digital entrepreneur. Today with the help of the internet, it is easier for anyone to start their own business. As Social Media is continuing to grow, more and more people are taking the entrepreneurial route.

TAB **25**

Online Business

You can start your own online business today!! Have you ever thought of starting your own Online Business? Or what is stopping you from starting your digital marketing, or becoming a Digital Marketer? It's not very complicated to start an internet or home-based business. First, you must identify the reason why you would want to start your own business. Remember your"WHY." Once again, your WHY could be anything personal that is going to propel you. Maybe you want to become financially freed, purchase a new Lamborghini, and so on. Always make sure that your WHY is strong enough because it's what's going to keep pushing you forward when you face some roadblocks and challenges.

One of the best ways to starting an online business or becoming a digital marketer is to joint venture with an already established company. You can become an Affiliate for that company and promote their product or services in return for a percentage commission. There are plenty of well-known companies and business sectors that offer these kinds of opportunities. Places like Best Buy, Amazon, eBay, Walmart, etc. have these incentive programs that are available to people who are willing to promote their products or services. It is usually free to open up an affiliate account with these companies. Once you open up an affiliate account, you'll get an affiliate link with banners or images of some of the products that you would want to promote. All you have to do is mainly to drive traffic to these products or services through your affiliate link. Once somebody clicks your affiliate link and makes a purchase, you'll get a commission. Chances are, you've probably shopped with some of these places regularly. You might as well go ahead and open up an affiliate account with them. Use your affiliate account for whenever you purchase something so that you can keep getting a small percentage of your money back. You can do the same thing for car rentals, hotels, airfare, etc. You can find these affiliate buttons at the very bottom of the homepage of these companies' websites. It should say something like become an affiliate or become a partner.

If you don't want to take the affiliate route, you can also come up with your business idea and keep 100% of the profits. You can do this by using the model that I called the Flows-hip of Digital entrepreneur. In this model, you would go through five phases into developing your Digital marketing business. These five phases are:

Phase1 is considered the Brainstorming Phase.
Phase 2 is Discovering your niche Phase.
Step 3 is Planning and packaging.
Phase 4 is Logistics.
Phase 5 is the Launch Phase.

Phase 1: This is the initial Phase or the Brainstorming Phase to determine what your business is going to be. As an Online Entrepreneur or a Digital Marketer, one of your primary objectives would be to solve problems or to get people or businesses from point A to point B. What issues could you be addressing right now? Although it takes a lot more research to determine a problem that needs solving, you can start with the basics. Start with yourself. Think of something that you are good at, and somebody else may be lacking. Think of things that you may be struggling with right now. All these could necessarily be potential problems that a large number of other people are also having.

Your other objective from being a Digital Entrepreneur is to provide value. Think of ways that you can be at service to others or how you can add value to the lives of others. Again you would want to start with the basics. Think of things that you are passionate about or things that you are just good at and how those things can be valuable to someone else. For example, you may be a positive minded person. You could use those attributes to help someone else potentially overcome some tough challenges. You could potentially become somebody else's lifeline. You may like going to the gym; you could think of becoming a Fitness Coach to help others. You could develope a course or a product arround all these things. Aside from yourself personally, you can also look at the domestic things around you. Think of your cell phones, cars, the lawn outside, think of kids, pets, etc. What kind of ideas or problems could you stem from any of those things that I've just mentioned? Let's take Cell phones, for example. What are the ways that cell phones can be improved upon? What are the problems that cell phone owners could be facing? What are related products or accessories to cell phones that you could be promoting? The concept applies to other things such as cars, homes, etc. Let's take the lawn as another example. With this, you could potentially start a simple business as a Lawn Mowing referral services. You could set up an agency arround these things. The point is there are potential business ideas all around you. You have to think in terms of solving problems or providing value to others. Even though these ideas that I've just mentioned are just examples and they may sound very simplistic or far-fetched. I'm here to tell you that those ideas have some great potential. These essentially could become a fortune. You have to develop the mindset of a person who can make all this possible. I highly recommend that you go back to the first chapter of this book and re-read it. There are inner workings of your mind that you must cultivate to develop these understandings. You must develop an internal representation of the things you wish to manifest outward. Simply put, if your goal is to become a millionaire, then you must become a millionaire before you become a millionaire. You cannot become a millionaire with a broke mindset. You are not inadequate because you have not. You are inadequate because your mind is inadequate. First develop a rich mind, develop a strong mind, then do whatever else after. Maybe start a business, be a superstar, or save the world whatever the case maybe for you. Never the less, Elite. If you are indeed looking to start a business, just know that there are business ideas all arround you. Start thinking in terms of solving problems or providing value to others.

TAB **26**

Start Right Now

Here is where you can start right now, today, at this very moment!. Go ahead and write down five things that you feel passionate about and can ultimately be in service to others. It can be anything like your hobbies and or your talents. You can also think in terms of basic human needs, such as comfort, safety, social, food, and shelter. Start thinking of ways that you can provide services or solutions to those needs. Once you've discovered a problem. You would be marketing the answers to this problem by using this model that I called the KBW diagram. In the KBW diagram. First, you would want to display the problem for your potential client. You would talk about the possible adverse effects of this problem. Then the next thing you would want to do is show the negative impact of this problem if it goes unsolved. After you paint this picture for your potential clients, then you want to introduce your clients to your solution to this same problem. You would want to offer them your miracle solution for the same problem. You want to show your clients the step by step application for your solution and potential benefits for using your product or service as the cure to their problem. You want to show them where they are right now while having this problem versus where they would be after applying your solution. See down below for an illustration of the KBW diagram.

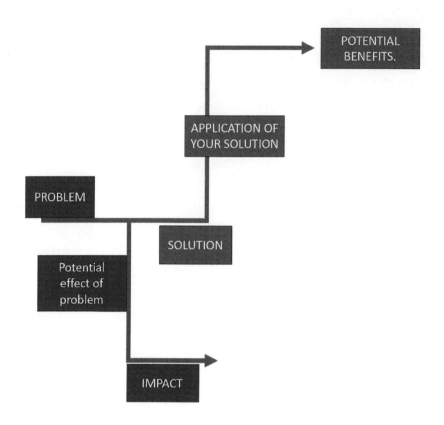

Phase 2: Discovering your niche phase. Once you've determined a Problem or a valuable idea that you want to market, this could essentially become your niche. A niche is a subset category of a broader category. For example, let's say that you want to go into the Fashion market. Your niche for that market could be one of the following: Maternal Clothing, Baby Clothing, Plus Size Clothing, etc. It is always good to focus on one specific niche to have a more direct brand so that you can quickly figure out your market. As you continue to grow bigger, you may want to cross-brand or expand on your niche to have a broader field. You want to make sure that there is a market or a demand for your niche; this is when a lot of groundwork and researching comes into play.

TAB 27

Research Your Ideas

Use those five ideas or problems that you listed in phase 1 for this example. Use google trends to research the trends for those five ideas. Things to keep in mind when conducting your research is that you want to know the seasonality of your objectives. Are your findings mostly trending in the Summertime or the Wintertime? What region of the world are your ideas most popular in? What are the age demographics for your objectives? Are Social media pages linked to your ideas? There is a Firefox or google chrome-extension tool call keyword everywhere that you can use to aid in your research. This tool would tell you the search volume or related keywords for a particular word or phrase that you search in google, using the google chrome or Firefox browser. You can use Facebook audience insights to help narrow down some of your ideas. You can also do an online survey. You can go to places like quora.com to ask questions in regards to some of your objectives. As an entrepreneur, you have to start thinking very creatively. You can go on Amazon and search for products relating to your ideas and see how many reviews there are for that particular product. The more the criticisms there are would tell you how people feel about that specific product or idea. You can use those criticisms to improve your products. Reviews and criticisms also provide insight into related products and services. As an entrepreneur, you reading customers' reviews, comments, complains, or concern can give you leverage as to how to make your product better than your competitors.

TAB **28**

Identify Your Buyer

As you continue to do this intensive research, start working on developing your buyers' persona. Your buyer's persona is a model used to determine who your ideal customer is going to be. You want to describe your buyers' persona in terms of their wants, likes, interests, age, hobbies, etc. Use a separate sheet of paper to outline your Buyer persona. For example, after a thorough research and discovering your niche. Let say that you were looking to go into the Physical Fitness niche. Based on your research, you found out that most of the people that are interested in your ideas or products are in the following:

Women, Age 24 to 65, Stay at home moms, mostly lives in Canada, the UK and the USA follow Fitness moms and Supermoms Facebook pages, interested in Physical fitness, tennis, yoga, belly exercises, etc. Your buyer persona would be something like this:

BUYER: Women
AGE: 24 to 65
LOCATION/REGION: Canada, USA, UK
FACEBOOK PAGES FOLLOW: "Fitness moms," "Supermoms," etc
INTERESTS: Home-based fitness, Belly exercises,
HOBBIES: Yoga, tennis,

Creating your buyers' persona can give you a lot of advantages. You are now able to address your potential clients directly. This helps when you are creating your advertising or writing your ad copy. For example, your ad may go something like: "Are you a stay at home mom looking for an effective home-based fitness program?" You can also use your buyer's persona to determine what kind of valuable content that you are going to produce for your potential clients. For the example above, knowing that your ideal buyers are interested in Belly exercises, yoga, tennis. You may want to produce content based on those things, such as tips for good belly exercise, hold a free live yoga session, etc. Taking this kind of approach allow you to build connection with your buyers and they can develop confidence and trust in you. Customers are more likely to buy form someone who they can trust.

TAB 29

Develop Your Product or Service

Phase 3: Planning and packaging

After you have discovered your niche, you are going to develop a product or service around your niche. It could be anything like a coaching session, selling a digital or a physical product, creating an online course, and so forth. Two questions to always keep in mind. 1) Are you interested in your idea? Or is it something that you are comfortable doing? 2) Is there a demand for this idea? Knowing the answers to those questions can help make things a lot easier down the road. Now that you've discovered your niche, or you've gotten a perfect idea that you are going to monetize. How are you going to develop that idea into a product or service that people are going to buy? This question is the part that most people get stuck at. First of all, you'll need to have some ethical considerations in mind. You are not trying to develop a business only to make money. You'll need to see yourself on the other side of the spectrum. Imagine you are the one that is going to buy from you. What would your expectation be for something in which you've invested your money? As an entrepreneur, one of your main goals is to solve the problem. With that in mind, you want to be able to show some contrast from where your potential clients are before they would buy your products and services and where they would be after they use your product or services. What kind of impact is your products or services is going to have on your potential End buyers? How are your products and services going to make your potential clients' lives better? Remember, these are people that are going to give you money, so you have to do all your due diligence. You may want to take some courses on the subject to have more authority or to increase your knowledge of the idea that you are trying to market. When you keep this picture in mind, then you'll able to go all out to create an impactful product or service. You'll price point your product and services based on the quality and the impact that is going create. There are two types of Newly Entrepreneurs. There is the Perfectionist, and then there is the Hesitator. The Perfectionist would want to wait until every piece in their business is perfect before they move forward with their business idea. The Hesitator is the one that's just scared to move forward. The Hesitator is afraid to take risks. One of the most significant factors that usually holds the Hesitator back is often timidness, or they are just scared to show their weakness to the world. They may say things like "I'm not a Camera Person," "I'm not good with computers." Elite as a beginner, it ok to be a Perfectionist or a Hesitator. I only want you to be aware of these two types of entrepreneurs and do not let neither one of them stop you from reaching your goals. Know that there are ways around these. Being a Perfectionist or a Hesitator are just stories that the conscious mind tells you for it to continue to be in neutral. One big reason why most entrepreneurs fail is that they go into business with an employee mindset, which means that they try to do every aspect of their business by themselves. They never think of hiring a coach, consultant, and things of that nature. Here is an illustration of how most entrepreneurs operate.

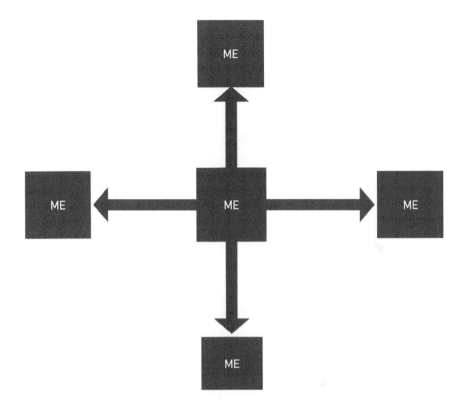

As you can see from the illustration above, it's all me, me, me. Most new entrepreneurs try to be the ones performing all the different operations of their business day in and day out. Doing this can becomes very overwhelming as time goes on. It is ok to do all the various tasks of your business if it doesn't require much. It is not to say that doing all the aspects of your business won't get you success, but the point that I want to drive home is that you want to create a balanced lifestyle and be very optimal. When you are at your optimal, you perform your best. You can make a better decision and feel good about yourself. As an Elite professional, this is one of the reasons why you must define your WHY in the early stages. If your WHY is to become your boss, then you want to start thinking like a boss. You want to dump out all those slaving or laboring mentality.

TAB **30**

Use Leverage

Imagine what an Elite boss means to you. You want to have time to do other things, like spending time with families or doing the things that you love. You want to meet those other areas in your circle of life. It's a good idea to know every aspect of your business, but you don't have to be the one doing all of them. It's ok to leverage some of the work to other professionals, and systems. Here is an illustration of the ideal model of how you want to conduct your business.

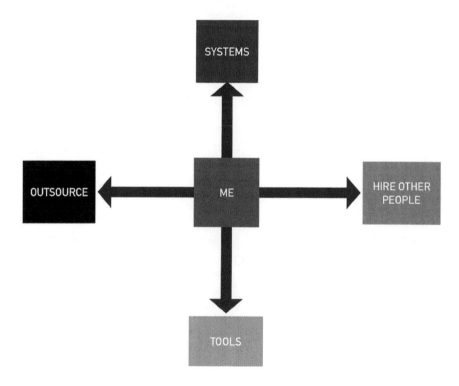

As you can see from the illustration above, you the Elite Boss; you want to be in the center of your business and oversees every operation. You can outsource or leverage other people's expertise. Unless your business would not be too complicated, then it would be alright to perform all the different tasks of your business single-handedly. If your business is very complex, then you would also want to put systems in place to help you perform specific tasks. For example, you may want to use autoresponders to send out batches of scheduled emails to all your potential prospects. If you were to create an explanatory video course but you don't feel comfortable getting in front of the camera. You can hire a professional video person to perform that task for you, or you can choose to do PowerPoints and voiceovers instead of videos. You can use fiverr.com to hire other people that are already comfortable and knowledgeable in these fields. Upwork.com is also an excellent source to hire people to perform specific tasks. As a new entrepreneur, it always advisable to hire coaches and consultants who are going help curve your mistakes and short-cut your success. You can go to different meetups events to start networking with people. Find someone who has already done what you are trying to accomplish and model after them. I also encourage you to go to various seminars and start interacting with other like-minded entrepreneurs. As you continue planning and packaging your business, start making all the necessary inquiries. Set aside your starting capital. Create a list of all the systems and things you would need for the operation of your business. Write the cost for each one of those things. The total of that cost is how much money you'll need to acquire to start your business. Get inspired in the process. Call some of the local brick and mortar businesses in your area.

Try to get an interview with the owner and see how they got started with their business. Ask them what their challenges were, how they got the money to get started, and so forth. Doing this will give you the idea, inspiration, and confidence to get started. Next, come up with an estimated amount for all your equipment, outsourcing, leveraging. The total sum for all those things would be your starting capital. The next thing that you want to do is to come up with a deadline to have your starting capital. You may want to start putting money aside or apply for credit card loans (progressive debt) to come up with your starting capital.

TAB **31**

Showcase Your Business

Phase 4 is the logistics phase: This is where your advertising, web hosting, and things of that nature all come into play. At this stage, you should have discovered your niche and decided what kind of product and services that you are going to create for your niche. During this phase, you want to determine how you are going to deliver your product or services to your potential buyers. You also want to start considering where you are going to house your product or services. For example, let say that you've made a course on how to lose weight. Your course may consist of stages of videos that show different techniques on how to lose weight. After you've made all these videos, you'll need a platform where you can host these videos so that your clients can access them at any time. One of the best places to host and sell your digital course is Udemy. Udemy is a popular market place where people go to search for things that they want to learn. It has a large community of students, entrepreneurs, and instructors. The great thing about Udemy is that it's a community and a marketplace. It makes marketing a little bit easier, and it doesn't cost anything upfront to start. Anytime somebody buys your course, half of the money goes to Udemy, and the other half goes to you. One of the most significant disadvantages with Udemy is that they have Price restriction. They control how much you will price your courses.

Another great platform to host your online course is Teachable. Teachable is free with its limited features. If you are looking to create a more professional course, then I suggest you get the paid version. The paid version allows you to have a customizable domain, generate coupons with an integrated email marketing. The basic pricing plan for teachable is $39 on a month to month, or $29 if billed annually. They also have a professional plan that goes for $79 and business plans that cost $399. The good thing about teachable is that they don't have a course price restriction. You can price your course to whatever you feel necessary. The only downside to teachable, compare to Udemy is that teachable is not a community based, or a marketplace. Which means you have to bring all your prospect to your course through some form of advertising. Here are other platforms that you can use to sell your course online: WizIQ, Rozuku, Thinkific, Coursecraft, Skillshare, etc.

If you were looking to sell a physical product or doing an E-commerce, then Shopify can be a great platform to use. Shopify has pre-built templates that allow you to be able to sell your Physical product and also your digital product to anybody and anywhere in the world. Most of those templates are free, but for some, you'll have to pay. You can customize your chosen templates with your business logo, and it also allows you to change the color themes, fonts, etc. You can upload images of the product that you are trying to sell, then add your selling prices, shipping prices, and so forth for that particular product. There are different applications or apps within the Shopify platform that you can use for different marketing approaches. One of these application is the Digital download application software that allows you to sell a digital product. Let say that you've created a written recipe that you would like to sell. The recipe can be in the format of Microsoft Word, Powerpoint, PDF, etc. The digital download app would allow you to upload that recipe into your Shopify shop so that people can download it for whatever price you set it. The app also keeps track of how many downloads you've gotten and your revenue.

You can also use Shopify for Drop-shipping; this is the most popular business model that most entrepreneurs use with Shopify. Drop-shipping allows you to sell products that you never have to maintain, store, or inventory, physically. The way that Drop-shipping work is that once you create your Shopify store, you can import different products from different vendors based on your niche market. The merchandise would already have vendor pricing. You can increase the prices in Shopify to create a profit margin for yourself. The main thing that you'll have to do is to drive traffic to the products or sell them. Anytime somebody purchases through your store, the vendor gets their money; they ship the product to your customer. You then keep the profit margin. In a sense, you are showing or selling the images of products to people. You never have to see or have the physical product on hand.

As you can see, Elite, there are a variety of different ways that you can store and move your product and services to your customers. It all just depends on the type of product and services that you are offering. As you continue to grow your business, you will become even more creative. You may do things like a one on one coaching; this is where you can contact your clients through telephone or skype. You can also do a mass group coaching through a webinar. Here is a list of webinars that you can utilize to reach your mass audience — Webinarjam, GotoWebinar, Getresponse, Zoom, Google Hangouts, etc. The good thing about doing one-on-one calls or webinars is that you don't need another external platform to house your course. Your contents would be delivered the same day to your Clients. This method would be good for consulting, if that's your niche.

Once again, Elite, Phase 4, is where you want to determine how you are going to deliver your products or services to your end buyers. You can choose to use one of the platforms mentioned above to house or deliver your content. You can also choose the hybrid method, which is just a combination of two or more of the above mentioned. After you've determined your product delivery method, you need to figure out two things.

1. How are you going to engage with your potential clients?
2. what kind of value are you going to provide to your potential clients to make them want to always buy from you.

Social media is one of the best ways to engage with your potential customers. You may want to create a Facebook page, Instagram, or a YouTube channel to engage with your potential clients regularly. You can provide value by giving tips and strategies, free giveaways, and doing product reviews, etc. You can also provide value by being inspirational or motivational. In most cases, the value that you provide should directly relate to the product and services that you are offering. Other times, the value that you provide can be indirectly related to the product or services that you are offering. The whole takeaway from this is that you always want to build some relationship with your potential clients, while you continue growing your brand. For instance, let's say that you were going in the Physical fitness niche. All the products and services that you are going to offer will be in this niche. Some value that you could provide to your potential clients would be one of the following: tips on a proper diet, how to do correct push-ups, and how to improve running, how to meal prep. You can also show before and after pictures of yourself. Share your journey of how you got in shape. You want to have a lot of engagements and keep your potential clients or your followers wanting more. As you continue to develop and focus on your niche, you may want to start thinking of ways to build your unique brand and have it stand out. You may want to come up with a unique name for your business, a mission statement, a logo, and a website for your business. Your business name and or your business logo would become your brand identity. When you are coming up with your business logo, you want to make sure it is something that sticks or something that people would always remember. You can put your business logo on coffee mugs, hoodies, and shirts to continue to push your brand identity.

Another big part of phase 4 is creating or setting up your sales funnel. Your sales funnels would look exactly like a funnel. It is wide and open at the top, then narrow at the bottom. This system allows you to capture as many potential clients, then filtering them down to the ones that are going to buy from you. These are the elements that you are going to need in your sales funnel. You'll need a lead magnet, a landing or a capture page, an email autoresponder, a one-time offer, and an upgrade. A lead magnet is something Free or valuable that you are going to give to your potential clients in exchange for their email address or contact information. The reason why you need your potential client's email address is that they may not buy from you the very first time they come in contact. Either they may not be in a position to do so at that very moment or simply because they haven't built any trust from you yet. Due to this fact is why sometimes a lead magnet can be very vital. A lead magnet is something of value, and it could be anything like a free book, a free PDF guide, coupons, a free course, free coaching, etc. A landing page is where your prospect would go to receive that lead magnet. A landing page is exactly like what it sounds. It's the first page where your prospect lands. A landing and capture page are essentially the same thing. Both landing pages and capture pages are action-driven. They both have a "CTA" or a Call to Action button that encourages the prospect to take a specific action. The main purpose of these is to get the prospect to convert, to become a potential client, or an actual paying client. The difference between a landing page and a capture page is that a capture page is shorter. A landing page is usually longer, and it's sometimes used to educate the prospect about the specific products and services offering. A landing page may have a short video about the specific product and service, then a call to action button that encourages the prospect to input their contact information. A capture page that is sometimes also called a squeeze page only does one thing, and that is to get the prospect's email or contact information. The prospect would have to click the CTA button and input their information to redeem the lead magnet. The boxes that pop up, where they can enter their information is the capture or the squeeze page. Once the prospect enters their email or information, they've now become your new lead. The email auto-responder is where your leads' information would be stored once they've entered it into your capture page. You are going to use the Email autoresponder to schedule a series of follow-up emails to your new leads. You want to get them to convert into paying clients or continue to build a relationship with them. After your prospects opt-in or decide to give you their email, they should automatically go to the next part of the sales funnel. The next part is the One Time Offer page or OTO. Your OTO page should have an Irresistible Offer or an IO. You've already done all your research. You've built up your buyer's persona. You know what your potential buyers are seeking. You know what kind of problem they are having. On your

One-time offer page, you are going to show them how your product or services is going to move them from where they are right now to where they want to be. Your Irresistible offer should answer the question of why they should buy from you. You are going to list all the things that they are going to get, including all bonuses, once they make the purchase. Your offer will be irresistible when its depicting problem solving, outlining bonuses, for a very reasonable price. You want to let them know that this offer will not be available at a later time, for the current price once they decline it. If they decline the first offer. You would want to show them a lesser offer. Maybe like a starter pack without all the bonuses at a lower price. If they accept the first offer and make the purchase, then you'll want to sell them a higher premium offer. For example, let say that you are selling a paid membership program with a lower, medium, and higher packages. A bronze, silver or gold packages. After your potential clients opt-in on your landing page, you'll redirect them to your middle packages or the silver package as the One time offer. If they decline that offer, then you'll offer them the lower or the bronze package. If they did accept the first offer, the medium, or silver package, then you'll try to offer them the higher or the gold package. You are trying to upgrade them for a lower price once they make the first purchase. The diagram below shows how a sales funnel should look. Your potential clients are going to go through this funnel, starting from you, providing tons of value to them. You'll then offer them the lead magnet. They would have to go to your landing page to get the free lead magnet. Once they are opt-in to receive that lead magnet, then you'll do a sales presentation or educate them more about your products and services. Once you've presented your products and services to them, then you'll give them an OTO (One time offer). If they accept the OTO and make the purchase, then you'll want to give them the option to upgrade.

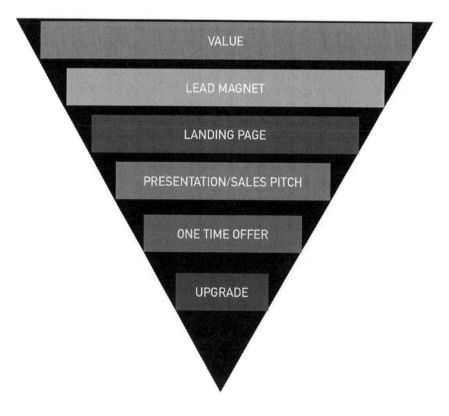

TAB **32**

Business Launch

Stage 5 is your launch phase. By this stage, you've brainstormed or researched great ideas or problems that you've also developed a niche around. You then take this simple idea and have planned it well then packaged it into a unique business. With all ethical considerations in place and have performed all due diligence, you've determined how you are going to move this business for profits. Now it is time to launch your new business out into the world. Launching for the first time can be one of the most exciting parts and can sometimes be the most frightening part for most entrepreneurs. Mainly because of not knowing what to expect. Elite, the first thing that you want to do is to remember all those mind-building principles that we talked about in Chapter one. The best way to look at the launch phase is that it is not a launch phase. Instead, it's the learning phase. Think of it as you are not launching your business in the beginning, but you are learning your business. First thing first, you'll need to be aiming for some metrics. So you want to have a goal that you wish to accomplish on your first launch. Yes, Elite! Write it down. It could be anything like the number of units that you wish to push for that day, the amount of traffic, customers, membership sign-ups, etc. Let's say, for example, on the day of launch; you are aiming to get 50,000 people to sign up for your product or services. What that means is that you have to show your product or services to at least 100,000 to 150,000. With the law of averages and the applied effort to reach 150,000, it gives you the probability to attain your goal of 50,000 sign up or more or within that proximity. Elite your day will not end until you make sure that you've shown your new product or service between 100,000 to 150,000 people. Consider Phase 5 as the birthing of your new product or service. It may take a lot of labor, patience, and pushing forward. You must continue to use metrics or goals throughout phase 5. You want to have data for everything. You are going to make a decision based on those data, not your emotions or feelings. After you've got your ideal goal, then you are ready for something called a Beta launch. In a Beta launch, you are going to price point your business at a lower margin or sometimes make it even free for a certain period. The goal for the Beta launch is to get as many people to know about your product or services. It is also to build trust and confidence. Those people who get to premier your product and services are the same ones who are going to help you sell your product or services and also help you improve your product or services. Here is an example. Let say that you've developed a product or a service that you were going to sell for $3,000. During your beta launch, you will want to price point that particular product to about $1,500 or so. Doing this allows more people to test your products or service as quickly as possible. Once you've got those people to test out your product or services, you'll reach out back to those same people to get feedback. You may want to ask them to do a product or service review, and this may be in the form of a video or written content. You may also want to ask for their permission to share those reviews with others. You are going to use those reviews to make your product better, especially the negative review. Some entrepreneurs sometimes think that negative reviews are always bad. Elite, as you go into becoming an entrepreneur, your main focus would be on matrices, numbers, and data. Try not to get too much of your emotions involved. If you get a lot of positive reviews, it's a good sign that your product or services are solving problems and or taking people or businesses from point A to point B. At the beginning of Phase 5, your launch Phase is still kind of like an experiment. You are still testing out your product or services to see how you could improve them. It is not calling for complacent but yet keep the wheels spinning. Going back to the above example. once the people who've bought your product or service for $1,500 have gone through to solve their problems. You will then reach back to those people and ask them for feedback. You are then going to take that data of information and use it to revamp your product. You may also use the positive feedback that you've gotten from your beta launch clients and use that as a method of social proof. Remember, people buy what other people buy. Most of the time, People want to get the result first before actually using the product or service. The only way that they can get that information is from someone who has gone through it. I called this the time travel effect of selling. It is one of the reasons why building a buyer persona is very critical. What you do is, once you've come to know the problem, wants, needs, likes of your ideal clients, then you are going to find a couple of people in real life that meet those criteria. You'll then have those people try-out your product or service for free, to transform their lives, or to solve their problem. You'll then have those people talk about their transformational experiences. so that when your ideal buyers see such transformation, they will feel like it them that have gone through that same experience, or they will feel like they've already gone through your product or services and are more inclined or easily influenced to buy from you.

Another thing to keep in mind is that you are not selling your product or services to your clients. Instead, you are selling them the result of having to use your product or services. You can do this through advertising. One of the best ways to illustrate this is by using a model called AIDA, which was developed by an American businessman named Elias St. Elmo Lewis in late 1800. The acronym AIDA stands for Attention, Interest, Desire, Action. Here is how the AIDA model works: You want to go through each letter in the acronym and make sure that the advertising for your product or services portrays each one of those letters. Let's start with the letter "A," which stands for attention. You want to make sure your advertising captures attention. In other words, make your AD an eye-catcher. Next is the letter in the AIDA model is "I" or Interest. Make sure that your AD generates some interest. You can do this by using numbers or by showing your potential buyers that you understand their problem. Share personal stories with them or personal stories of other people who have gone through your product or services. Here is an example of how to capture interest using numbers: "Eight out nine men do XYZ." "90% of women do XYZ." People are more likely to want to get more information on a subject that involves stats. Here is an example of an advertising headline that captures interests by showing that the advertiser cares or understands the pain of their potential customer. "Trying to lose weight, but not getting any result? I know exactly how you feel "or "you are not alone." The statement shows what the potential client is going through and how your product/services are going to help them.

The next letter in the AIDA model is D for Desire. With this, you'll want to entice your potential buyers with the desire to buy your product or services. Show them the solution to their problems. Show them how are they going to accomplish or go from point A to point B. The final letter in the AIDA is A, which represents action. In this step, you'll want to get them to take a specific action. It always a good practice to use a no-obligation statement like "learn more" instead of "buy now." When you are creating your advertising for your product or services, or when you are making a sales pitch, you always want to sell the idea of having your products or services. What it'll feel like to have your product or services. For example, if you were to sell some shoes. You don't want to say things like buying these shoes for such and such price. Instead, you want to say how comfortable it is to have the shoe on. How the show can make a person walks better or runs faster. These are the kind of ways that you would want to angle your sales pitch or advertising for your product or services.

TAB **33**

Your First One Million

Most people aspire to make a million, but they've never broken it into small achievable steps that are going to get them there. Elite, here is a breakdown of how you are going to earn your first $1,000,000. First of all, there are over 5 billion people in this world. All you have to do is influence one million of those people to each give you $1. The question is, what are you going to give to get? What kind of value are you going to provide for those people, for them to want to award you with $1? Think creatively, Elite. There are so many other ways to reach a million. Here are some few examples:

You will have to sell a $20 product or service to 50,000 people.

Sell a $200 product or service to 5000 people.

Sell a $500 product to 2000 people. Sell a $1000 product to 1000 people. Sell a $2000 product to 500 people. Sell a $4000 product to 250 people. Get 5000 people to pay you $17 a month subscription for 12 months.

Get 2000 people to pay you $42 a month subscription for 12 months.

Get 1000 people to pay you $83 a month subscription for 12 months.

Get 500 people to pay you $167 a month subscription for 12 months.

Get 250 people to pay you $333 month to month subscription for 12 months.

With this in mind, what kind of product or services are you going to create? Think Elite!

There you have it, Elite! You can make something of yourself, and you don't have to settle for the status quo. This book should serve as a guide to invoke the creative powers within you. Study yourself. Know the exact lifestyle that you desire, and go for it. You may not get it right on the first try but continue to push and fail foward. Fail your way to success! Find someone who've done the things that you are trying to accomplish and model after them. Get a coach or a mentor. The road to success is a one-way street. You can only go forward. If you try to go the opposite way, your life may get even harder. When you decide that you are ready to go after success or change your life for the better, know that you may face some setbacks, doubts, series of temporary defeats, nobody would believe in you. You might lose some friends in the process; you may get hurt, your pets may die, you might lose your house, you may go through a breakup or a divorce, your electricity may get cut off. Things may happen. Life may throw everything at you to test you, to make you stronger, to build you up, to make you become a new person. I'm not trying to sound too cynical, but I'm saying, Elite, you may face some challenges, but you must keep pushing forward Elite because You have been empowered, from the information that you've read! Now it is time to go graduate from this YOUniversity.

Monday, May 27th, 2019, Midnight. There I was sitting in my office room surrounded with a bunch of positive messages on the wall. I've read through and performed the various tasks in this journal entries. I put all these into the book that you are holding. My imagination has been running wild.I feel like I've flashed forward and outlined the roadmap for my success before it'll happen. This is the information that you are holding. I feel very refreshed. The past couple of months of doing these journal entries has been very therapeutic for me. I must say that I feel very empowered now. I have so much clarity. After putting into practice all the things mentioned, especially in chapter one of this book. I have realized that it was me all along. I was the one holding the key to my prosperity and my deterioration. I have considerably discovered myself, the power in me! I wrote this book for me, but I wrote this book for you. As you continue to develop your **SELF**, you'll also produce some of these

Eccentric new attributes. Always try to include some

Mediation into your daily routine.

Pray for strength, pray to have some dynamics as you go through life!

Overcome whatever obstacle that comes your way as there will be some.

Write down your goals, your aspirations, your affirmation, and your gratitude.

Exercise daily and eat well.

Read self-help books, read inspiring stories, read your affirmations and read out your goals and

Expect good things to happen to you, because it will. Last but not least

Develop courage and devote yourself, and you will become very SELF-EMPOWERED!

Made in the USA
Middletown, DE
21 March 2022